Best
TEA SHOP WALKS
in
SURREY & SUSSEX

Margaret & Barrie Howard

D1639026

Published by Sigma Leisure – an imprint of
Sigma Press, 1 South Oak Lane, Wilmslow, Cheshire SK9 6AR, England.

British Library Cataloguing in Publication Data
A CIP record for this book is available from the British Library.

ISBN: 1-85058-588-1

Typesetting and Design by: Sigma Press, Wilmslow, Cheshire.

Cover: Arundel Castle from the River Arun

Maps and photographs: the authors

Printed by: MFP Design and Print

Disclaimer: the information in this book is given in good faith and is believed to be correct at the time of publication. No responsibility is accepted by either the author or publisher for errors or omissions, or for any loss or injury howsoever caused. Only you can judge your own fitness, competence and experience.

Contents

The Walks

Summary of Walks

WALK	LOCATION	DISTANCE	TEASHOP	DESCRIPTION
1	Godalming	5 miles	Boat-house	Easy. Towpath, woodland, fields, historic town. Two climbs.
2	Compton	4¼ miles	Large converted barn	Easy. Country lanes, fields, North Downs Way.
3	Shere	6½ miles	Traditional	Moderate. Undulating fields and heathland. Lovely views.
4	Abinger Hammer	4 miles	Country teashop	Moderate. North Downs Way. Superb views. One steady climb.
5	Ranmore	5 miles	Converted farm building	Moderate. Fields, woods. Superb views. Some climbing.
6	Fetcham	5 miles	Converted barn in working farm	Easy. Norbury Country Park. Lovely views.
7	Merstham	3½ miles	Farm teashop	Easy. Woods & fields.
8	Woldingham	9 or 5¼ miles	Traditional	Strenuous. Steep ascents & descents. Downland, woods, spectacular views.
9	Lingfield	5 miles	Traditional	Easy. Open fields, Lingfield old town.
10	Alfold	4¾ miles	Farm shop & cafeteria	Easy but can be very muddy. Woods, fields, towpath.
11	Mytchett	5¾ or 3¼ miles	Traditional. Visitor Centre	Easy. Woodland, heathland, towpath.
12	Hindhead	4¼ miles	Cafeteria	Strenuous. Devil's Punch Bowl, Gibbet Hill. Panoramic views.
13	Haslemere	5¼ miles	Traditional	Easy. Fields, woodland. Medieval moat.

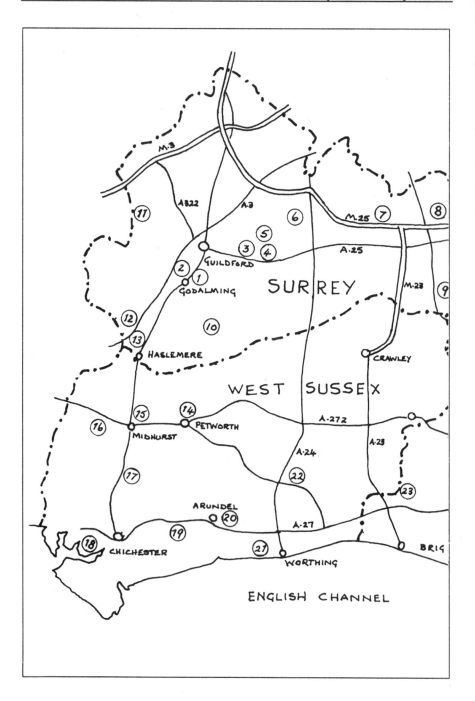

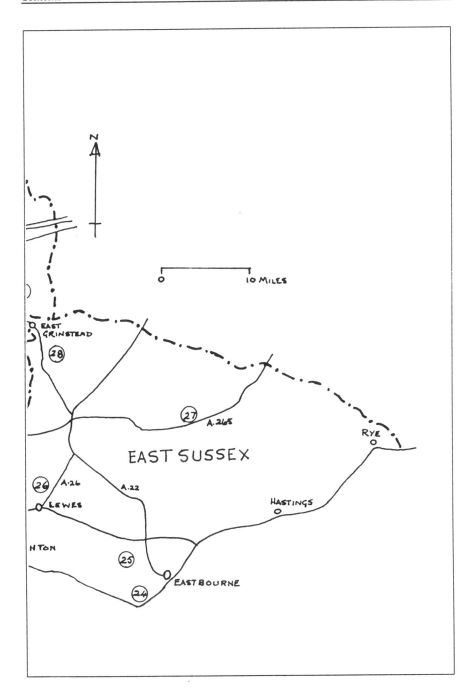

Key to symbols used on sketch maps

Path on route	– – →
Path not on route	▪ ▪ ▪ ▪
Road	═══
River	∿∿∿
Pond, lake or sea	⬭
Church	✝
Tea Shop	⊤
Viewpoint	⩊
Trig. point	△
Windmill	🜨
Point in text	②
Building referred to in text	▬
Public House	P.H.

Introduction to Surrey & Sussex

The counties of Surrey and Sussex are much more than over-crowded commuter belts for the City, fast track lanes to airport and ferry terminals or large country estates in splendid isolation behind high walls. Waiting to be discovered, a footstep away from this hectic activity, is the peace and quiet of long winding country lanes, miles of ancient hidden footpaths in the two most wooded counties in the country and acres of beautiful undulating and tranquil countryside.

The Downs and Weald of Surrey and Sussex comprise a vast acreage of rolling countryside. Villages and hamlets, lost in a time-frame of yesteryear, are set on hillsides and in river valleys. Myriads of footpaths traverse ancient woods and heathland. Wildlife is abundant and it is not unusual for a walker to disturb deer, spy a fox or maybe even a badger. Pheasants roam the woods and fields, occasionally startling the walker with their sudden flight for safety.

Traversing the springy turf of the Downs, there is the anticipation of spotting rare orchids, finding Britain's largest snail, the Roman Snail, in the Downland grasses or hearing the skylark as it flies high on the wing.

More than 10,000 miles of footpaths and bridleways, give a lifetime of walking permutations. Long distance footpaths traverse the North and South Downs: link paths across the Weald enable the real enthusiast to make a round trip over both Downs of over 250 miles. A more gentle walk of 105 miles can be undertaken along the Greensand Way, crossing the Greensand hills for the first 55 miles between the pretty towns of Haslemere and Limpsfield, then on for a further 50 miles to Ham Street on the northern edge of Romney Marsh.

For those who prefer less arduous walking, this book aims to provide pleasant rambles along lesser used footpaths, allowing time on the way to enjoy the history and beauty of the countryside.

The landscape of the Downs and Weald has changed over millions of years. As far back as 135 million years ago rivers flowed from the surrounding land bringing with them Wealden clays and coarse-grained sediments that settled into a vast freshwater lake.

Further changes occurred twenty million years later when the sea broke into this area. With every change of tide, the Lower Greensand, Gault Clay and Upper Greensand were tossed and turned on top of each other, becoming deeper as time passed. Slowly the climate became warmer and drier, rivers flowed less and the sea became clearer as chalk slowly accumulated on the bottom as sediment containing minuscule sea shells and marine plants to form a layer 1,000 feet (over 300m) thick.

Eventually, violent movements of the earth caused the gradual folding and uplifting of the sea bed into a long domed formation. The chalk reached its greatest height in the Central Weald, pushing and weakening the earth in the surrounding areas to open up fissures which exposed older sands and clays. The rivers, winds and hard winters slowly eroded the overlaying chalk and Greensand from the central portion of this great dome to reveal the Wealden clay. The chalk edges of the north and south escarpments are all that is left of the great central dome: they are the Downs we see today.

Below the North Downs of Surrey lie the Greensand Hills; below the South Downs of Sussex is the less obvious Greensand Ridge. The Greensand rock formation follows the line of the Downs in an arc. At the western end they form picturesque hills with many beautiful viewpoints: Gibbet Hill, 892ft(272m); Blackdown, 918ft(280m); and Leith Hill at 965ft(294m), the highest point in the South-East.

Between the Greensand Hills and the Greensand Ridge lies the fertile clay and sand of the Weald. This Wealden clay supports a thriving agriculture: wheat fields, fruit orchards and sheep farming are the mainstay of the farming industry, whilst expanding acreage of vineyards indicates that viniculture is now becoming a profitable industry.

Around the time of the first Roman occupation of Surrey and Sussex the forests stretched for about ninety miles. The Iron Age was in its infancy at this time but as it developed it was to have a dramatic effect on the forest landscape. The industry was at its height during the sixteenth and seventeenth centuries when half the iron mills in

England were situated in Surrey and Sussex. However, by the eighteenth century the realization that too much timber was being taken for charcoal burning and the competitive development of coalfields in the north caused the industry to decline.

Small ponds found today in the woods and villages may be old 'hammer ponds' used in the iron industry. These ponds, some still showing their different levels, provided a head of water for driving the waterwheels, which in turn powered the iron beating hammers.

During this period an additional impact on forests was the use of timber for furnaces for the glassmaking industry. Eventually a Royal ban was put on the use of timber for firing the furnaces and this industry also declined.

Approximately 10,000 years ago most of the heaths of Surrey and Sussex consisted of lightly wooded areas dominated mainly with a mixture of oak and beech. Tree felling for rough grazing opened up large areas of this woodland: these open spaces plus the acidic conditions of the Greensand soils favoured plants such as heathers, gorse, bilberries and bracken. In times past these plants were used as household material: heather and gorse for kindling, bracken for floor covering and both heather and bracken were used for stuffing mattresses.

Heathland provides a valuable habitat for many species of flora and fauna: a diversity of plant-life includes the Common and Dwarf gorse and Ling and Bell heathers; the many birds breeding on heathland include stonechat, woodlark, tree pipit and hobby.

In recent years, the cessation of grazing, which led to the domination of birch and bracken, increased conifer planting and the introduction of rhododendron, have all contributed to the drastic reduction of our heathland. The loss of over four-fifths of heathland during the past two hundred years has led to the diminishing of a large quantity of diverse and valuable wildlife. Today, management teams are working to prevent further decline. Much of the young birch is now pulled before it can take hold. In order to correct the balance, in a natural and economical manner, between strong plants such as bracken and scrub and the weaker heathers, cattle and ponies are once again being put to graze on many of the commons.

The beauty of the landscape of Surrey and Sussex is greatly enhanced by the rivers meandering gently through the villages and towns. Initially, they do not appear to have taken the line of least resistance to the sea, which is to run parallel with the Downs escarpments: instead they have cut deep gaps through the Downs to reach the River Thames or the English Channel. The reason for this can be traced back to the long mountain dome of many centuries ago which formed a watershed.

The River Ouse cuts through the narrow but lofty chalk Downs about five miles from Lewes, then winds through meadows to the port of Newhaven. Looking down from Lewes towards the Downs one wonders how this slow running river pushed its way through the 500ft(152m) high walls of chalk Downland.

The River Arun, linking with the western River Rother at Pulborough, meanders lazily across water meadows, enters a gap at Amberley and flows freely past Arundel and its castle to the sea at Littlehampton.

The Adur joins the sea at Shoreham, whilst the Cuckmere, the most easterly of these four rivers cleaves a narrow gap into the sea below the South Downs, without port, harbour or village.

The two main rivers in Surrey are the Mole and the Wey which rise in the Weald and cut through the North Downs on their journey to the Thames. The Mole, a picturesque river, has cut a dramatic gap through the North Downs leaving behind steep cliff slopes rising up to Box Hill.

From 1600 onwards various Acts of Parliament were passed allowing the rivers to be made navigable: initially little progress was made as mill owners objected to water being transferred from the rivers to operate the locks. Eventually in 1800 the River Ouse was made navigable between Lewes and Lindfield and in 1816 the Rivers Wey and Arun were linked by canal to extend trade links from London to the south coast. These navigations, although initially successful, were eventually surpassed by the coming of the railway.

Many artists and writers have been inspired by the beauty of Surrey and Sussex. Helen Allingham (1846-1926) was born in Derbyshire but spent most of her married life in Surrey. She is best remembered for her idyllic portrayal of country-life through her paintings of thatched cottages, country gardens with their profusion of flowers and barefoot children at play in the sunshine.

J.M.W. Turner spent long periods at Petworth House in West Sussex, under the patronage of the Third Earl of Egremont. He painted prolifically during this period and his many landscapes include those of Chichester, Brighton, Tillington church, and the lake and sweeping lawns of Petworth Park. Many of his paintings and sketches can be seen in Petworth House, a National Trust property open to the public.

William Cobbett lived in Farnham as a child, returning there in his later years. It was after his journey of exploration across the south-east on horseback, that he wrote Rural Rides, a study of the life of agricultural workers in the 1800s. Whilst his writings showed his heartfelt compassion towards the rural poor, they also conveyed his deep appreciation of the beauty of the English countryside.

Much of the land we enjoy walking on today is in the ownership of the National Trust. The Trust was founded in 1895, by three far-sighted conservationists – Robert Hunter, Octavia Hill and Hardwicke Rawnsley, in order to "preserve places of historic interest or natural beauty permanently for the nation." The first property acquired by the Trust was Dinas Oleu, a four-and-a-half-acre cliff top given in 1895 by Mrs Fanny Talbot. The first building to be purchased was the almost derelict Clergy House in Alfriston; it cost £10. In 1906 Mr Hunter, concerned at the rate at which local land was being suburbanized, raised funds to buy 750 acres of Hindhead Common. He also instigated the acquisition of Box Hill and several other popular open spaces. By the outbreak of war in 1919 the Trust owned sixty-three properties covering 5814 acres, twenty-eight of which had been gifted. After the war many more gifts of land were made in memory of the fallen. In the 1930s the Trust began to establish its position as the preserver of stately homes and gardens. Today, one hundred years since its formation, the Trust has become Britain's largest private landowner: whether rambling along the wooded slopes of the North Downs or climbing a mountain in the Lake District, one cannot help but feel a debt of gratitude to the Trust's dedicated founders.

In the early hours of 16 October 1987 a hurricane occurred which, in a matter of a few hours, drastically changed a landscape which

had taken hundreds of years to mature to its present splendour.
Winds of well over 100 miles an hour swept across southern Britain
from the Channel Islands. Houses were devastated, church spires
toppled, caravans, lorries and even light aircraft blown over and
more than fifteen million trees were completely uprooted. On National Trust land alone 250,000 trees were blown down. So great was
the devastation that initially it was thought most of our magnificent
woods and stately gardens were damaged beyond repair. However,
landowners such as the Forestry Commission and the National
Trust plus a vast army of volunteers fought back with energy and
imagination. The opportunity to remove old and damaged trees was
taken, new plantings took place, views which had been opened up
for the first time in hundreds of years were maintained and natural
regeneration was encouraged. So remarkable has been the effort
that, ten years on, it is possible to see that the trees and woodlands so
crucial to the landscape of Surrey and Sussex will, in years to come,
be fully restored to their former magnificence.

The Tea Shops

A warm welcoming tea room on a cold winter day, or a sunny tea garden on a warm summer day – what better way could there be to end a
not too strenuous ramble?

Tea shops being few and far between in the countryside, we felt,
when we decided to write this book, that combining a good walk
with not only a tea shop, but one that welcomed ramblers, would be
quite a challenge. However the challenge proved to be most reward-
ing: some of our discoveries are quite unusual and many of them are
well off the beaten track.

From Fanny's Farm Shop to the rather grand tea room in Fitzhall
Manor House, all our tea shops welcome ramblers, muddy boots ex-
cepted of course! Most will appreciate advance notice of the in-
tended arrival of a walking group. The majority of tea shops not only
offer homemade fare, they also have that 'little something' extra that
adds so much to the atmosphere: it may be the attractive gift shop
within the premises; the local produce for sale; the ducks and hens

running around the garden, or quite simply a personal welcome from a friendly hostess.

With two exceptions all the tea shops are open throughout the day and serve both light lunches and afternoon teas. All but two have outside seating, most of which is in very attractive gardens.

As the majority of the tea shops are individually owned, opening hours can be a little erratic – especially in winter; therefore, a telephone call before persuading the family to leave the fireside on a cold winter's day could possibly save a lot of disappointment!

The Walks

The twenty-eight circular walks range from 3½ miles to 9 miles and are suitable for anyone of reasonable fitness. We hope they will appeal to the seasoned rambler wanting an easy day and to those new to rambling seeking encouragement to explore further afield.

The walks are all graded and range from the only totally flat walk along Bosham Harbour to the more strenuous challenge of The Downs. Surrey and Sussex although not mountainous, do have gentle hills and undulating countryside, therefore even the flattest of walks is almost bound to have some 'ups and downs'.

For good support and personal comfort lightweight walking boots are recommended. They are especially useful in cattle grazed wet meadows and on the Downs where the chalk paths can be very slippery. Carrying wet weather gear is a sensible precaution and a flask containing a hot drink adds enjoyment to all but the shortest of walks.

The maps referred to are the Ordnance Survey (OS) Landranger series 1:50,000 (1¼ inches to 1 mile) and Pathfinder and Explorer series 1:25,000 (2½ inches to 1 mile). All the footpaths are on Public Rights of Way or Permissive Paths (paths where the owner permits public use). Sketch maps are numbered to correspond with the instructions in the text and should be sufficient for your needs. However, an OS map will give a more detailed description of the surrounding area and identify features not mentioned in the text. An OS grid reference is given to locate the start of each walk, the numbers apply to either map. The walks have been checked but please note that stiles and gates can fall into disrepair and footpaths are occasionally re-routed. Please inform your local Ramblers Association Group if you meet any obstructions or diversions.

Additional information is included on interesting places and features passed on the walks – we hope you will be encouraged to allow time to stop, look and listen to, the sights and sounds of our delightful countryside.

PUBLIC TRANSPORT

Where possible the names of public transport operators have been given. For further information contact the operator referred to at the beginning of each walk.

Bus services

Autopoint Coaches	01323 832430
Brighton & Hove Buses	01273 886200
Arriva	01737 223000
London General	0181 646 1747
Nostalgiabus	0181 640 6668
R.D.H. Services	01273 890477
Stagecoach (Coastline)	01903 237661
Stagecoach (Hants & Surrey)	01256 464501
Stagecoach (South Coast)	01424 433711
Tillingbourne Buses	01483 276880

Train services

All train inquiries	0345 484950

1. Godalming and the River Wey Navigational Canal

Route: This walk along well defined footpaths is fine for any season, even after rain the towpath is relatively dry. Two steady climbs have attractive views on their descents. The route goes through the old market town of Godalming.

Teashop: The Riverside Tea Room at the back of Farncombe Boat House is on a slip of land between the river and the canal. There are seats outside for watching the bird life and boats whilst enjoying afternoon tea. Open April – September, Thursday – Monday 11.00am – 5.00pm and weekends in winter 11.00am – dusk. Tel: 01483 418769

Distance: 5 miles.

How to get there: Godalming is 4 miles south west of Guildford on the A3100.

Public Transport: Bus services: Stagecoach Hants & Surrey, Stagecoach Coastline, Tillingbourne. Trains: South West Trains.

Start: GR 971440. Crown Court Car Park. Free Sundays only.

Maps: Landranger 186, Pathfinder 1225 SU84/94, Explorer 145

1. Walk back through the car park to the road. Cross over and turn right to walk parallel with the river. Shortly join the riverside path on the left which turns diagonally right and passes the public library. Exit on to the Town Bridge and cross to the United Reform Church. Pick up the riverside path on the right of the church and with the Lammas Lands on the left continue along to Catteshall Lock.

The Lammas Lands date back to the days of communal farming. Bread baked with corn from the first harvest was consecrated at a special Thanksgiving Mass on 1 August. Hence 'Loaf Mass' which eventually became 'Lammas'.

The Wey & Navigational Canal, from the River Thames to Guildford, was completed in 1653. In 1764 the waterway was extended to Godalming with the opening of the Godalming Navigation. Godalming prospered as barge traffic became increasingly popular: by the early 1800s beer, corn, wooden goods & many more products were being transported to the London markets. Although by the end of the century bargees were facing the competition of road and rail transport, it was not until 1969 that commercial traffic finally ceased.

In 1996 the National Trust replaced the old gates of Catteshall Lock with new ones made from English oak; they also re-instated the tow-path using material dredged from the canal.

2. Leave the canal by the gate on the bridge and turn right into Catteshall Road. Cross by the old engineering works on the left to continue along the old section of the road, passing Brocks Close and Warramill Road on the left. Turn left into Catteshall Lane then right at the Ram Cider House.

The Cider House was built in the late 16th century as a high quality Hall-House. In the 1300s houses were built with a large central hall open to the rafters with smoke vents in the roof. By the 16th century upper floors were created, a narrow section being left open to form a smoke bay. Later, brick chimneys were built within the smoke bays. The Cider House still retains many of its original features. At the corner of the road opposite the Cider House and set in the wall is a hydraulic water-ram. Installed in the 1920s it is thought to have been used for the gardens of Catteshall Manor.

3. Steadily climbing, the road bears left and continues up alongside the long garden wall of Catteshall Farm. It then becomes a wide track leading up through open varied woodland, passing Violet Wood and Lane Cottage. On reaching Munstead Heath Road turn left. This is a busy road so keep well in to the verge. After a quarter of a mile take a footpath on the right at a walled driveway to houses, passing a beautiful old house named Orchards.

Sir Edwin Lutyens is Surrey's most famous architect. Born in London in 1869 and brought up in Thursley village he later moved back to London from where he practiced. His first important commission occurred at the age of 20 when he designed Crooksbury, a nine-bedroomed house near Farnham. Recognition of his talent grew and in 1897 he designed Orchards one of his finest masterpieces. Built of Bargate stone its many

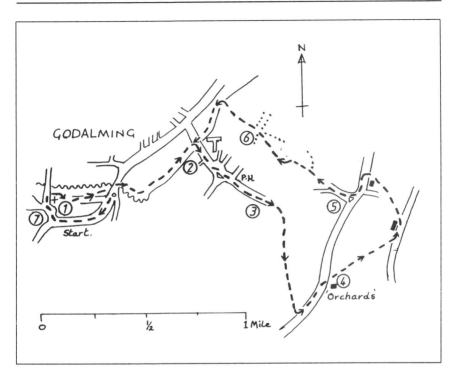

fine architectural features include the wing containing the carriage house and stables and its magnificent tall red-bricked chimneys. The terraced gardens were designed by Gertrude Jekyll. In 1919 Lutyens was asked to design a memorial for the nation: the simplicity and elegance of the Cenotaph established his reputation world-wide.

4. Keep ahead over three stiles, gradually descending between fencing to the road at Nurscombe Fruit Farm. Turn left and after 100 metres turn left again onto a bridleway which climbs to Wood End House at the road. Turn left. Go past Munstead View Road then cross to Unsted Park Lodge.

5. Walk up the drive and as the drive bears left at a gateway take a bridleway alongside Unsted Wood. When the path bears right keep ahead through a kissing gate. The footpath descends between fields. Where the path forks left at a house on the left keep ahead to a crossing path at a three-way signpost.

6. Approximately 25 metres beyond the signpost turn left (there is a white house to the right). Continue along the path to reach the canal. Cross the bridge and turn left to follow the towpath back to Farncombe Boat House and the tea rooms. Continue along the towpath to Town Bridge, cross to Bridge Street and at the end bear right into High Street to walk through the town.

Godalming is an historic market town. The Greensand hills surrounding it and the river running through have both contributed to its prosperity. The hills with their light soils have always provided good grazing for sheep farming. From the River Wey came the power needed by the mills, first for the production of woollen cloth in the medieval period, and later by the frame knitting, paper-making and tanning industries.

Once an important staging post between London and Portsmouth, Godalming was visited by Peter the Great of Russia in 1698 when he stayed at a coaching inn on the site of the present King's Arms. This patronage was a mixed blessing for the landlord as it soon became apparent that the vast quantities of food and drink consumed by the Tsar and his entourage were unlikely to be paid for! The present King's Arms was built in 1753. In 1814 the landlord of the time was host to the Emperor Alexander I of Russia and King Frederick William of Prussia.

In 1881 Godalming became the first town in the world to have electric street lighting: the power for the generator coming from the River Wey. Initially the system was not a huge success and in 1884 the town reverted to gas until the equipment was perfected. A plaque in the old Market Hall commemorates the event. The Hall built in 1814 is at the centre of the three main streets, a small open-arcaded octagonal building it is affectionately known as the Pepper Pot.

The part-Norman parish church, built of locally quarried Bargate stone, is on a beautiful site between the High Street and the river. An exceptional feature for this part of England is its impressive 150ft (45m) lead spire.

7. From the Pepper Pot turn right into Church Street, Turn right at Borough Road to the Phillips Memorial Cloister on the right.

This memorial was erected in honour of a local hero, John George Phillips, chief radio operator of S.S. Titanic, who remained at his post sending out Mayday signals as the liner sank in the Atlantic on 15 April 1912. Ger-

The tea rooms

trude Jekyll who designed and planted the memorial garden is one of the country's most famous garden writers and designers. Born in 1843 she lived at Munstead Wood, Godalming. An advocate of planting flowers in drifts, using subtle contrasts and simplicity of design, her theories have influenced generations of gardeners. A great friend and patron of the young Edwin Lutyens she designed many of his gardens. Today the names Lutyens and Jekyll are synonymous with all that is finest in house and garden design in west Surrey.

8. Continue along the riverside path. This short walk under the willows is quite beautiful, especially in springtime. After about 180 metres you will see the car park on the right.

2. Compton, Loseley Park and the North Downs Way

Route: This is an easy and interesting walk through Compton village, down quiet country lanes and across open countryside. There are many interesting features. The paths for the most part are well made tracks making it a good all-season walk.

Teashop: The Tea Shop in Watts Gallery is renowned for its homemade cakes, quiches and soups. There is seating outside. Open daily 10.30am – 5.30pm (closed 2 weeks Christmas). Tel: 01483 811030

Distance: 4¼ miles.

How to get there: From the A3 south of Guildford take the B3000 to Compton, turn left at the roundabout and first left into Down Lane. From Godalming take the A3100 and turn at the B3000 to Compton. From the village turn right into Down Lane.

Public Transport: Bus services: Stagecoach Hants & Surrey, Tillingbourne.

Start: GR 955477. From Down Lane take the first turning left signposted 'North Downs Way'. Parking will be found near the road bridge.

Maps: Landranger 186, Pathfinder 1225 SU84/94, Explorer 145

1. From the car park walk back to Down Lane, turn right to return to the junction with the B3000, visiting Watts Chapel en route.

Compton's most famous resident was Mr G.F. Watts a Victorian artist and sculptor. In 1895 when part of Budbury Hill was purchased for use as a burial ground, he and his wife wished to ensure the beauty of the spot was maintained. The chapel, designed by Mrs Watts, is built with bright red brick and decorative terra-cotta in the shape of a Greek cross. The circular room is startlingly decorated in Art Nouveau style with paintings of children, cherubs, flowers and mystic symbols. Above the altar hangs a painting 'The All-Rewarding' by Mr Watts. Watts himself paid the entire cost of the chapel; many parishioners helped with the building and art work. Behind the chapel is the cloister where Watts is buried: the ceme-

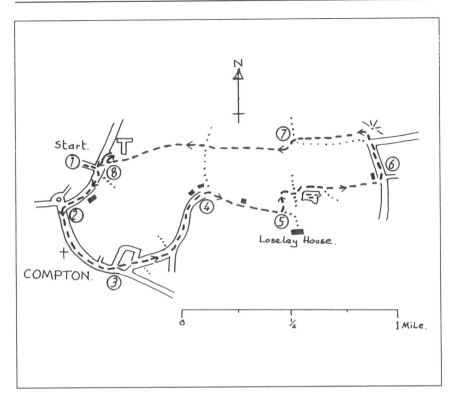

tery contains interesting headstones inscribed with beautiful Victorian epitaphs.

2. Turn left along the main road to walk through the village, passing cottages, antique shops, and The Harrow public house.

Despite its proximity to the A3, Compton, once a stopping place on the Pilgrims' Way, still retains a rural charm. Along the main street are some beautiful cottages, the most unusual of which is the timber-framed White Hart Cottage built on a high bank above the road. Set on a hill above the village is the church of St Nicholas, said to be one of the most beautiful and interesting small churches in England. Part-Saxon, its features include 12th century murals, an ancient hermit's cell, and a unique sanctuary with a carved wooden rail which is claimed to be the earliest example of Norman carpentry in a church in England. Set in the Norman window behind the altar is a beautiful representation of the Madonna and Child.

3. At the telephone box in Spiceall Road go diagonally left across a recreation ground towards the trees on the right of some houses and take a road ahead. Ignore a footpath to the right after about 70 metres and on reaching a road junction keep ahead passing a No Through Road sign.

4. Just beyond Polstead Manor take a footpath on the right opposite Little Polstead. Continue on this path, passing a small cottage called Polstead Lodge, until reaching a stile at a three-way signpost, at this point the road becomes a private road to Loseley Park.

   Loseley House, set in magnificent parkland and built with stone from the ruins of Waverley Abbey, is a fine example of Elizabethan architecture. It was built for, and is still lived in by, the family of Sir William More. Queen Elizabeth I, James I and Queen Mary were all visitors to Loseley. The farm is now famous for its herd of pedigree Jersey cattle and Losely cream products. The house, garden and farm are open to the public from late May to the end of August, Wednesday to Saturday plus Bank Holidays. For details ring 01483 304440.

5. Turn left over a stile. Follow a path down over two stiles and turn right at the field edge. Cross a stile, a track and another stile to enter a field. Follow the footpath through the field to a stile at the end of the lake. (From this field there is a fine view of Loseley House.) Cross the stile and continue ahead through three fields to Littleton Lane.

6. Turn left by the picturesque Pillar Box Cottage on the corner and continue to the junction with Sandy Lane. Continue ahead to go through a gateway (the view on the right is towards Guildford) then turn immediately left at a waymarker post onto the North Downs Way (acorn sign) and continue ahead.

   The Hog's Back (A31) high on the right of the track was once an old Drove Road with the earliest reference to its use dating back to Saxon times. It is said to have been used by King Alfred on his journey to Winchester and later by the Pilgrims on their way to Canterbury. However it is generally accepted that the section of the North Downs Way covered in this walk was the main Pilgrims' Way. Being a much lower road it would have provided a more pleasant path with leafy shelter in the summer months.

7. Where the track joins a track from the right, turn left then immediately right for a steady climb between trees. At a waymarked crossing continue ahead. Eventually a farm is passed which sells fresh produce and free range eggs, in the fields on the right of the farm grazing deer may be seen. This footpath leads back to Down Lane, with the welcome sight of Watts Gallery and the tea shop on the corner.

Watts Memorial Gallery houses many of the paintings, drawings and sculptures of G.F. Watts. During the war it was considered sufficiently remote for the safe storage of many pictures and treasures from the London galleries. However as a necessary precaution the roof was covered with camouflage paint and a spotter plane sent up to see if the gallery could be seen from the air. The pilot returned to say that the gallery had been undetectable.

8. Turn left then first right to return to the parking area. If you look up as you walk under the bridge you will see a large cross on each side denoting the route of the Pilgrims' Way.

The Watts Chapel

3. Shere and Sutton Abinger

Route: A pleasant, not too strenuous walk from a delightful village to a pretty hamlet. The route climbs through the Tillingbourne valley and across open undulating fields and heathland with lovely views en route.

Teashop: The Lucky Duck Tea Room is a delightful half-timbered Lutyens' building and was originally a barber's and boot-maker's shop. Today, it is a charming, traditional teashop gaily decorated in bright yellows and blues, its tables set with fresh, crisp lace tablecloths. There is plenty of extra seating in a lovely secluded garden. The menu offers an extensive range of food, from sandwiches to a three-course meal and a delightful assortment of homemade cakes and scones. The tea room is open daily from 10.00am-5.00pm. Closed Christmas and New Year. Tel: 01483 202445.

Distance: 6½ miles.

How to get there: Shere is just off the A25, approximately halfway between Guildford and Dorking.

Public transport: Bus service: Tillingbourne. Trains: Thames Trains. Nearest station: Gomshall.

Start: GR 074480. Park at Shere recreation ground behind the village hall. If arriving by train, begin the walk at Twiga Lodge in paragraph 2.

Maps: Landranger 187, Pathfinder 1226 TQ04/14, Explorer 145 & 146.

Nestling in the Tillingbourne valley, protected by the North Downs, with a delightful duck-filled stream flowing under the High Street and pretty Wealden and Lutyens houses; it's little wonder that Shere is described as one of Surrey's loveliest villages.

In the 1880s, the promising young architect Edwin Lutyens was courting Helen, daughter of Sir Reginald Bray, the Lord of the Manor, and was therefore a frequent visitor to Shere. Sadly, the courtship failed, but Sir Reginald gave Lutyens several architectural commissions. East Lodge in Upper Street, the Lychgate at the church, the building which now houses the tea room and the forge next door are all beautiful examples of Lutyens early works.

Sutton Abinger

The 12th-century Parish Church has many interesting features and is well worth a visit. There is documentary evidence that in 1329 a young girl Christine Carpenter, wishing to prove her chastity and obedience to God, obtained permission from the Bishop to have herself walled up in a tiny cell in the church. Christine came out for a brief period but after three years she returned to her cell and, although not proved, it is thought she died there. The squint and the aperture through which food was passed to Christine are in the north wall.

Over the centuries, Shere has attracted the attention of many authors and painters: J.M.Barrie, Henry James and Helen Allingham were all inspired by its beauty. Cobbett, riding through, observed it to be 'one of the prettiest rides in Surrey'. Today the village is busy and bustling, yet it still retains an air of friendliness and charm.

1. From the car park return to the road, turn left then right along Middle Street, passing the tea room on the right. Cross the stream,

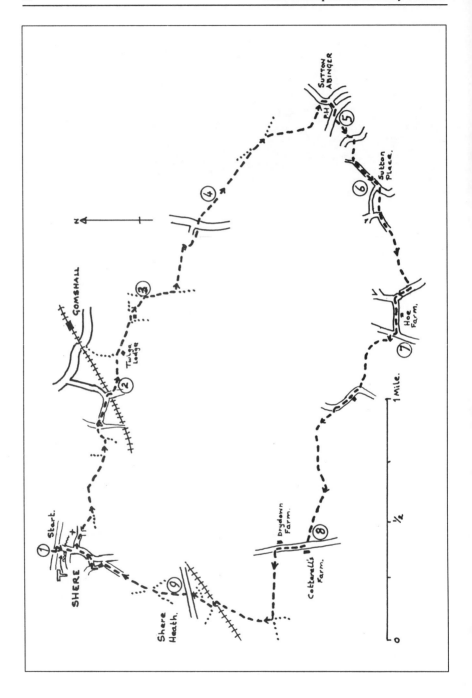

turn left into The Square and continue to the Parish Church. At the junction of Church Lane and Church Hill, take a path uphill to a gate into a field. Pause to enjoy the lovely view back across the valley then turn left along the field boundary. Pass through a further gate and gently climb between fencing. Ignore a path on the left by some garages and soon reach a junction. Turn left then right to a road. Cross straight over and turn left along High View. On reaching Tower Hill, pause to look at Malthouse Cottages on the left, then turn right under the railway.

Malthouse Cottages are the result of three periods of building. The centre cottage, the oldest part of the building and once a hall-house, bears a plaque dating the building at 1526. The gable on the left, added in the 17th century, has elaborate half-timbering with curved braces. The right-hand gable is much plainer and is possibly 18th century. Although these cottages have lost most of their original land to the road and railway, they still retain character and charm.

2. Sixteen metres beyond the bridge turn left to Tower Hill Farm and take a narrow path alongside the boarded fence. At the end of the fence, bear left alongside a wire fence. Turn right onto a broad gravel track, immediately passing a house 'Twiga Lodge'. On reaching Southbrooks Farmhouse, turn left at a bridleway sign. Ignore a fenced path at the end of the farm and enter a field to cross it diagonally right.

3. Turn right onto a footpath (Rad Lane). After 70 metres turn left to go over a stile then immediately right along a field edge. On reaching a signpost turn left and go straight across the centre of the field to a stile. Over the stile turn right for a few metres then left to descend to a road. Cross over to a stile into a field. Turn right, cross a footbridge and climb between fencing, past Oxmoor Copse, to a stile at the top of the field.

Oxmoor Copse is a gift to The Woodland Trust. It comprises three acres of ancient woodland which, before the storm of 1987, was predominantly oak. In 1996, the Trust completed a replanting programme. In order to encourage a greater diversity of wildlife, ancient woodland trees of oak, ash, wild cherry, crab and rowan were planted.

4. Cross the stile and follow a line of electricity poles diagonally across two fields; follow the field edge for 50 metres then pass through a wide opening on the left. Turn right for a few metres, then left at the field edge and follow the electricity poles again down the field. At the end of the field (there is an electrical transformer on the right) turn left down a sunken path. The path soon changes to a wide track and leads to a road (Raikes Lane). Turn right to walk through Sutton Abinger.

Nestling in the Greensand Hills at around 500 feet (152m) this lovely hamlet must be one of Surrey's best kept secrets. A photographer's delight, it consists of 3 half-timbered houses and one public house, all at least 400 years old. The hillside garden of the pub, The Volunteer, has a superb view across the valley.

5. Follow the road round on the right to Horsham Road. Turn right and after 40 metres cross over to go up some steps and over a stile for a steady climb between fencing. Turn left at Stile Cottage. After 25 metres turn right: keeping the gardens on your right continue ahead to a road. Turn left along the road.

6. Immediately beyond a T-junction where there is a Sutton Place House Plan turn right along a footpath. Keep ahead at a road, passing houses on the left then follow a track to a stile. From the stile descend between two fields then climb to a stile into a field. Cross the field (you may see Llamas in an adjacent field) to a driveway and the road. Turn right, passing Keepers Cottage and continue to the junction at Franks Field. Turn left, pass Hoe Farm on the left, and continue downhill to a road.

7. Cross over, turn right then left onto a fenced path through Peaslake Nursery. Cross a stile into a field and follow a right-hand hedgerow to a stile into a second field. Cross directly over heading for a stile in the left-hand corner. Cross the stile and turn right along a lane. Sixty metres beyond Oak Farm turn left into a field. The path turns right then curves gently left across the field to a kissing gate, to a road. Cross over to a broad track and gently ascend alongside a right-hand field boundary. At the top of the field, continue on a fenced path which gradually descends to the road and Cotterell's Farm.

8. Turn right along the road: take care this busy road has no pavement. Pass a small lake on the left then reach Drydown Farm. Stay on the road until reaching the end of the farm buildings then turn left into a field. Follow a broad track straight across this large open field to a line of trees on the far side. Immediately on reaching the trees, find a narrow path which drops down to a stile, two steps and a sunken crossing path. Turn right along the sunken path and soon emerge at a lane and houses. Continue to the last house and turn left over the level crossing. Keep ahead for 15 metres then turn right onto Shere Heath. Follow the main path as it twists and turns across the heath, keeping ahead at a crossing path en route.

9. On reaching a road cross directly over onto a wide path and continue across the heath, ignoring all paths off. The path soon descends and merges with a path left then right just before reaching a waymarked fork. Here take the right-hand path which ascends for 15 metres then gradually descends to a road. Continue ahead to the last house (no.31) then bear left along a narrow path. Cross a driveway, pass through a barrier and continue to a road. Follow the road round as it turns right to the main road. Turn left into Shere. Pass Shere Museum on the left, The Square on the right and continue along Middle Street to the tea room. Turn left at the end of Middle Street to the recreation ground.

---

4. Abinger Hammer and the North Downs Way

Route: This pleasant walk over the Downs is not difficult but it does include a steady climb at the start and one steep scramble of 15 metres. The descent down a rutted track could be unpleasant after heavy rain. Its attractions are the superb views to the Greensand Hills and the discovery in their seasons of wild flowers native to the chalk of the North Downs.

Teashop: The smell of home baking, fresh crisp table linen and friendly welcoming staff combine to make the Clockhouse Tea Rooms on the village green one of our favourites. All the cakes and pastries are homemade, our capacious teapot for two yielded three cups each, and the moist carrot cake and chocolate shortbread were quite simply superb. There is a small garden with a view to the green. Open all year 10.00am – 5.00pm (closed Monday). Tel: 01306 730811

Distance: 4 miles.

How to get there: Abinger Hammer is on the A25 between Guildford and Dorking.

Public Transport: Bus services: Arriva, London General, Tillingbourne.

Start: GR 096474. Turn off the A25 opposite the Post Office onto the B2126. The small village car park is in front of the offices of Martin Grant.

Maps: Landranger 187, Pathfinder 1226 TQ04/14, Explorers 145 & 146.

The clear water of the Tillingbourne river, the attractive village green and the famous overhanging clock all contribute to draw in many visitors to Abinger Hammer. For over 200 years the valley rang with the noise from a large water-driven power hammer used in the working of iron. The unique clock on Clockhouse corner was first erected in 1891 and has existed in its present form since 1909; given in memory of the first Lord Farrer of Abinger Hall, it also commemorates the connection of Abinger Hammer with the iron industry. The Tillingbourne, once dammed to provide hammer ponds for the industry, is now more famous for the excellent watercress grown in its clear chalk beds. The watercress is not only sold locally – it is also served daily as a speciality in the Clockhouse Tea Room.

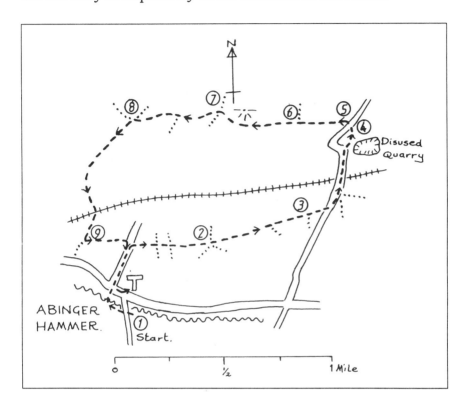

1. From the car park cross the village green to a footbridge in the far corner. Cross the A25 at the Clockhouse Tea Rooms and turn first right for a steady climb up Hackhurst Lane. After approximately a quarter of a mile at the brow of the hill turn right onto a bridleway: the lovely views from this track are to the North Downs. Go through a gate, across a track and onto Broomy Down.

2. At a junction of five paths continue ahead bearing slightly left. The bridleway leads through The Roughs, bears left along the edge of Abinger Roughs and eventually reaches a tall granite monument.

The Wilberforce monument

This monument marks the spot where Samuel Wilberforce, Bishop of Winchester and son of William Wilberforce the abolitionist, died on July 19 1873 after being thrown from his horse. The horse had stumbled when catching its foot in a rabbit warren.

3. From the monument continue along the track to a road. Cross the road and turn left, cross the railway bridge and after approximately 230 metres turn right onto a footpath. After a few metres turn left in front of a metal gate and follow a narrow path up between trees. The path soon opens out and from the clearing a disused quarry can be seen below.

Flint and chalk were mined from this quarry. The flint was used for local building purposes; lime was made from the chalk for use in mortar and fertilizer.

Wild flowers thrive in the chalk of the Downs. The hairy violet and sweet violet brighten the Downs in March when little else is to be seen. Many species of orchids can be discovered in the summer: towards the end of the season the autumn gentian makes its appearance. Two of the many butterflies are the Adonis and the Chalkhill Blue: you may see Britain's largest snail – the Roman Snail.

4. After a few metres turn left for a short steep scramble up a narrow chalk path. At the top of the hill is a spectacular view across the valley to the Greensand Hills. Swing round to the right onto a narrow path between trees leading to a road.

5. Cross the road onto the North Downs Way. As the path curves you pass the first of three pillboxes to be seen on this walk.

Concrete and brick pillboxes were built as a defence chain across the south-east of England in the 1940s in readiness for a land invasion: fortunately their effectiveness was never put to the test. Ironically, it is since the end of the war that many of these Pillboxes have been destroyed. In order to protect those remaining and as part of a Defence of Britain survey they are currently being collated and mapped by the Surrey Industrial History Group.

6. The path leads through White Down Lease, open woodland on the left allows lovely views of the Greensand Hills. Just before leaving this section of the Downs there is a wooden bench to ad-

mire the view in comfort towards the village of Holmbury St Mary and Holmbury Hill.

Well over a hundred years ago the peaceful hills we look across to provided refuge for smugglers, sheep stealers and bandits. Contraband was hidden in the cottages below and the area was known as the wildest in the county.

In 1872 the Victorian architect George Edward Street and his wife, visiting the village which was then called Felday, fell in love with it and had a house built there which they named Holmdale. In 1879 Mr Street designed and paid for the building of the parish church of St Mary. The village acknowledged this benevolent gift by changing its name to Holmbury St Mary.

7. From White Down Lease continue ahead, first onto Blatchford Down then through a gate onto Hackhurst Down.

8. Keep with the NDW as it turns left through a kissing gate then bears right to a further kissing gate. Here leave the NDW and turn left down a broad track. This track is now extremely rutted due to four wheel drive vehicles using it for leisure purposes. It descends to lead under a railway bridge then past a large entrance gate to commercial greenhouses.

9. Fifty metres beyond the gate turn left onto a narrow footpath then left again (in front of a wooden gate) to walk along the edge of Piney Copse. Cross a stile and a field (which may be muddy after rain) then cross another stile to arrive back at Hackhurst Lane. Turn right to the Clockhouse Tea Rooms.

---

5. Polesden Lacey Estate and Ranmore Common

Route: This walk through woods and open fields is particularly lovely in late spring when the woods are carpeted with bluebells. There is a little climbing but it is amply rewarded by the fine views across the landscape. The route includes a visit to Polesden Lacey (NationalTrust).

Teashop: The tearoom, gift shop and an excellent plant stall are all to be found in the Stable Courtyard at Polesden Lacey. The menu offers morning coffee, homemade lunches and afternoon teas. There is an excellent assortment of homemade cakes. Open April to October daily 11.00am to 5.00pm. February, March and November, Wednesday – Sunday until 4.00pm. Tel: 01372 456190

Distance: 5 miles.

How to get there: From the A246 between Guildford and Leatherhead take the turning to Greene Dene. After approx. half a mile, turn left into Crocknorth Road, signposted to Ranmore Common. Three-quarters of a mile beyond the Effingham/Abinger crossroad, turn left into Stoneyrock Road. The car park is a quarter of a mile along the road on the left.

Public Transport: None.

Start: GR 124505. Ranmore Common Car Park, Stoneyrock Road.

Maps: Landranger 187, Pathfinder 1206 TQ05/15, Explorer 146

---

1. From the car park turn left along the main road for 100 metres. Turn left along a wide track (just in front of a lone white cottage). The track soon narrows between fences then descends between holly trees to a house on the left. Walk up the drive to a road and cross onto a drive opposite. Where the drive bears right, turn left over a stile. Follow a wire fence down a field to a stile. Continue down a grassy path to a road. Cross diagonally right to a footpath through a wood. Continue through the wood, with fields on the right and crossing two stiles. Immediately over the second stile

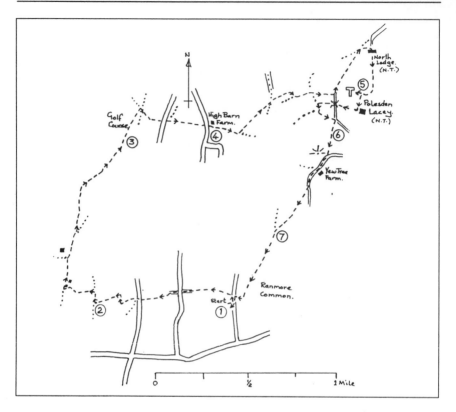

bear right to cross a further stile. Turn left alongside a wire fence, pass through a gate onto a bridleway.

2. Turn right for 100 metres then turn left over a stile to go down a field and into a wood. On reaching a timbered house 'The Old Malt House' turn right along a bridleway. On reaching a house 'The Studio' turn right. Where the path forks take the left path: this lovely path meanders between oak, beech, birch and coppiced hazel; follow all the yellow waymarkers until emerging at a golf course.

3. Follow the waymarking signs across the fairway to the 12th tee at a wood-chipped footpath. Turn right and pick up the waymarkers again, crossing two fairways to a footpath behind gardens. At a road cross onto a footpath and bear left to cross a stile by a gate. Follow a field boundary on the right to High Barn Farm.

4. Cross the road and with the stables on the left take a bridleway through woodland to a stile on the left by a gate. Cross a field and a stile. Follow the footpath first round then through a wood to emerge at a wide track coming from the left. Bear right: as the track curves right there are fine views towards Ranmore. At a crossing path cross into a field, turn right and follow the footpath round to Yew Tree Lane. Turn left along the lane and follow it round to North Lodge. Turn into the Polesden Lacey grounds and follow the footpath parallel with the main drive to the Stable Courtyard and the tearoom.

Although there are references to a house on the Polesden Lacey estate as early as 1470, the present house was only built in 1821. Its most famous owner was the Honourable Mrs Ronald Greville, the daughter of the Right Honourable William McEwan, MP for Edinburgh and founder of McEwan Breweries.

Mrs Greville and her husband bought Polesden Lacey in 1906 to consolidate their position in the highest levels of society. Edward VII was entertained here and Mrs Greville received her highest accolade when King George VI and Queen Elizabeth accepted her offer of Polesden Lacey for their honeymoon.

The house is beautifully situated on high ground, with fine views to

Thatched bridge, Polesden Lacey

Ranmore Common from the south terrace; to the east are the steep slopes of Box Hill. The estate consists of over 1300 acres of ancient woods, historic farmsteads, rolling downland and scenic pastures. In order to maintain the present pastoral landscape intensive farming is not allowed and the farmland is used mainly for grazing purposes.

At the request of Mrs Greville; Yew Tree Lane was re-routed in the 1860s away from the house so that tradesmen would be less visible. The pretty thatched bridge was then built so that she could walk from the rose garden to the kitchen garden without going into the lane below.

5. From the tearoom turn right towards the house then turn right again through the Walled Garden. Cross the thatched bridge to the summer house then turn left along the Former Kitchen Garden to a lane. Turn left along the lane for approximately 150 metres. Turn right onto a bridleway: after a few metres the path steadily ascends.

    The spoil from the sunken lane was used to make this embanked path which when planted with yew trees became known as Yew Tree Walk. During the storms of 1987 over 30 acres of the estate's woodland was destroyed. The loss of many trees along Yew Tree Walk caused the subsequent erosion of the footpath. Ten years on, clearance, replanting and natural regeneration has taken place throughout the estate. In 1996 with the help of a National Trust volunteer group a clearance and replanting scheme was successfully completed on Yew Tree Walk.

6. Turn right to continue uphill to Yew Tree Farm. From the viewpoint there are lovely views down Polesden Valley to Box Hill. At this point the bridleway forks but stay on the main bridleway for 140 metres to a right fork at a wide gate and stile into a field. Keep to the top edge of the field until reaching a signpost then bear right down the field to a stile and a track.

    This track skirting Ranmore Common is called Hogden Lane: the old meaning of Hogden is Valley of the Pigs. This suggests the lane was once used as a route for driving pigs to the common to forage.

7. Turn left along the track which climbs gently and passes two cottages on the right. At the end of the second cottage turn right onto a narrow footpath ('no horses' sign here) which leads to a lane. Turn left for 100 metres to return to the car park.

6. Mole Valley and Mickleham

Route: This is an easy walk for any time of the year. The footpaths are well-marked, there are some fine views and the Mole Valley is always a pleasure to walk in.

Teashop: The Old Barn Tea Shop is in a converted 18th century barn on Bocketts Farm Park, a working family farm with old and modern breeds of animals. There are newborn animals and fowl on show plus displays and demonstrations. All the meals are cooked on the premises – their fresh, warm scones are particularly recommended. Open every day from 10.00am – 5.00pm, but closed for two weeks mid-January. The Farm Park is very popular during holidays and at week-ends, it may be best to avoid it at these times. Tel: 01372 363764

Distance: 5 miles.

How to get there: From the M25 exit at junction 9 take the A24 Dorking Road to the A246. Bocketts Farm is a quarter of a mile on the left.

Public Transport: Bus services: Arriva pass within 1 mile. Trains: Nearest station Leatherhead 1 ½ miles.

Start: GR 156549. Bocketts Farm Car Park, Fetcham.

Maps: Landranger 187, Pathfinder 1206 TQ05/15, Explorer 146

Norbury Park Estate was bought by Surrey County Council in 1930. In 1766 much of the woodland was lost when magnificent walnut trees were cut down for use as gunstocks for the British Army. In Victorian times the estate was extensively managed for pheasant rearing. Today a gradual renovation is taking place: softwoods planted in the 1970s are being replaced with beech, oak, yew and hornbeam; currently there are plans to increase the quantity of hazel, which takes up to fifteen years to mature, for coppicing. On the estate are three tenant farms Norbury Park (dairy) Swanworth (sheep) and Bocketts Farm Park.

1. From the car park turn right onto a bridleway. At the second signpost turn left then immediate right through the wood, keeping

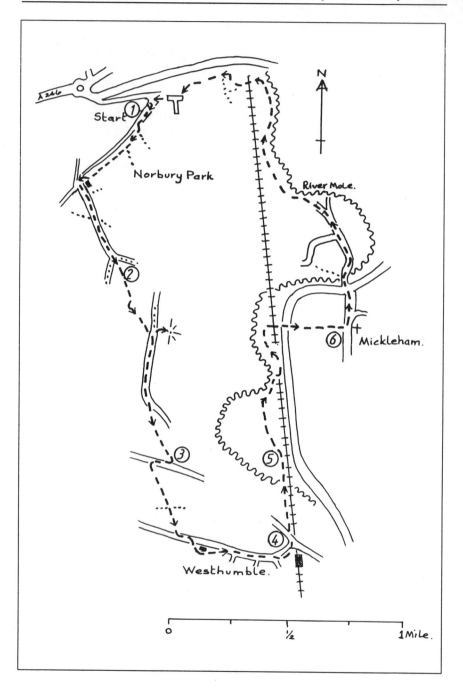

parallel with the bridleway. When the footpath starts to climb to the left, turn right to descend to the bridleway at a brick building. Continue for about 50 metres to a crossing path and turn left towards Westhumble.

2. Ignore all paths off until reaching a three-way junction. Take a bridleway uphill into a wood. The path winds through the wood until reaching a road. (Across the clearing to the left are extensive views to Box Hill and Mole Valley.) Turn right along the road. Where the road turns left, bear right onto a bridleway.

3. From Crabtree Lane car park turn right to the first signpost. Turn left over a stile (The view here is to Ranmore Church) then diagonally left down a field to another stile. Follow the footpath down to go over (and through) a stile. Cross a track into a field and keeping a wire fence on the left walk down to a lane. Turn left to the Chapel Remains. Turn right onto a bridleway then left down a fenced footpath to rejoin the lane. Turn right to walk to Crabtree Lane (it is possible to use the pavement from Pilgrims Way). Cross by the Archway dedicated to Fanny Burney.

Fanny Burney, born in Norfolk in 1752 and once a royal attendant to Queen Charlotte, established herself as a novelist whilst living in Surrey. It was as a guest at Norbury Park that she met and fell in love with General Alexandre d'Arblay, one of a group of monarchists who had fled the French revolution: they later married at Mickleham Church. Two of her most well known works are the novels Evelina and Camilla.

4. Just before the railway bridge turn left onto a footpath. Keeping the railway on the right go down a field and across a footbridge over the River Mole.

Norbury Mansion can be seen on the horizon. Built in 1774 and in private ownership, its views were claimed to extend as far as the centre of London. Previous owners include Thomas Grissell who, in 1848, allowed the railway to pass through the estate on condition it was hidden from view; Leopold Salomons, one of this country's first conservationists, who in 1914 bought Box Hill and presented it to The National Trust and Dr Marie Stopes, the family planning pioneer who lived there for some years until her death in 1957.

5. Go through a gate then diagonally left across a field to a further gate and a footpath at the side of a cottage. The footpath leads past some farm buildings and Cowslip Cottage then under and back under a bridge and eventually to Swanworth Cottages. Carefully cross the main-line level crossing and the main road to rejoin the footpath. This path leads to Mickleham village.

Mickleham church

The church of St Michael is a lovely building dating largely from the Norman period. Although reconstructed in 1842 evidence of this earlier period includes the font and the fine entrance into the chancel which has late Norman windows. More recent features of the church include a rare Flemish stained-glass window, a beautiful sculptured portrait of Queen Victoria and a memorial window to Canada.

The 17th century Running Horses Inn was once used for stabling horses when racing at Epsom.

6. Turn left down to the A24. Cross to a bridleway at the bridge. The bridleway leads past Mickleham Priory to a fork where you take

the path left. Approximately 100 metres before a house on the left turn right at some wooden stumps to go through an opening in a wire fence. Follow the river for a few metres then turn diagonally left up a field and through a gate to continue on the main path into a field ahead. Cross the bottom of the field to a gate by the river. Turn left to go through a tunnel and up a few steps on the right. Go through a gate and follow a path up a field. Just beyond a green marker post turn right at a large beech tree. Walk between the trees then turn left up the field to a stile and footpath leading back to Bocketts Farm and the Old Barn Tea shop.

```
┌─────────────────────────────────────────────────────────┐
│                                                           │
│   7. Upper Gatton Park and Mugswell                       │
│                                                           │
└─────────────────────────────────────────────────────────┘
```

Route: This is an ideal walk for a lazy afternoon. It is mostly flat, in springtime Upper Gatton wood is carpeted with bluebells.

Teashop: Fanny's Farm Tea Shop is a tiny extension of the main shop but there is plenty of seating in the attractive country garden where you may find yourself in the company of ducks, geese, hens or Vietnamese Pot-bellied pigs! Homemade chocolate cake and fruit pies are Fanny's speciality. Open every day from 8.30am – 7.00pm. Tel: 01737 554444

Distance: 3½ miles.

How to get there: Leave the M25 at Junction 8 to take the A217 to Reigate. Turn first left to Merstham. After approximately one mile turn left under the motorway into Markedge Lane. Fanny's Farm Shop is half a mile along on the left.

Public Transport: None.

Start: GR 544277. Fanny's Farm Shop.

Maps: Landranger 187, Pathfinder 1207 TQ25/35, Explorer 146

The Lodge, now Fanny's home and once the gate house to Upper Gatton House, was built early this century by the estate workers of Sir Jeremiah Coleman – of mustard fame. Between 1935 and 1945 the Lodge was used both as a gate house and a prison. In 1948 Gatton Park became a poultry farm, the three sheds alongside the Lodge being used for the poultry. The Lodge and the old farmsheds have now been converted into Fanny's Farm Shop. A founder member of A Taste of Surrey, Fanny sells fresh vegetables, homemade cakes and local produce plus antiques and Victorian-style cotton nightdresses!

1. From the car park turn right along the road for approximately 50 metres. Turn right onto a bridleway alongside the vineyard. Go through a gate and across a track into a field. Cross the field, turn left in front of a stile and gate to follow the field edge then cross a stile into Upper Gatton wood. Where the path forks take the right path, immediately passing a footpath on the right. Turn left at a

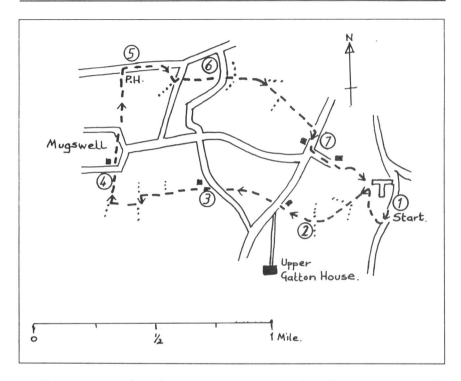

T-junction and within 10 metres turn right, after approximately 30 metres go past a pillbox (see walk No 4) to cross a stile into a field.

The original Upper Gatton House, once lived in by Sir Jeremiah Colman's daughter, was burnt down in 1930. It has been said that the butler caused it with a discarded cigarette! The house now standing was rebuilt from the stable block and servant's quarters which fortunately survived.

2. Keeping the wood on your right go down the field, passing another pillbox and Upper Gatton House over to the left, to a road. Turn right and cross the road opposite a house named Pilgrims. Cross the stile, go straight across a field then bear left following the hedgerow up to a stile in the far corner. Cross a road to rejoin the footpath by Keepers Cottage.

3. Follow the footpath through fields, passing a wood on the right, then cross a stile at the bottom of a field. Turn left for approxi-

Fanny's Farm tea shop

mately 100 metres then right at a metal gate to walk up the edge of a field. Turn right at the top and leave the field by a stile in the top right hand corner. Follow the footpath down to a road.

4. Cross the road to continue on the footpath which leads behind houses and across a further road (May Cottages) to a stile. Continue ahead across two fields and down the side of a wood to Chipstead Lane and the Well House Inn. Turn right.

   The Well House Inn built in the 13th century has a timber-frame infilled with knapped flint stone. At a time when there were very few about, the inn was originally built as a coffee house. The well in the garden bears the following inscription "This well is credited as being the original St Margaret's Well or Mag's Well (hence the name of the area Mugswell) as is mentioned in the Domesday Book. It is probable that St Margaret's Well was the original settlement of Celtic or Anglo-Saxon herdsmen."

5. Initially the lane climbs, as it starts to descend cross a stile on the right into a parking space. Cross a stile on the left and continue diagonally right across a field to the road. Turn left then almost im-

mediately right over a stile into a field. Cross the brow of the hill diagonally left to a stile at the end of a line of conifers. Follow a footpath to a road.

6. Cross diagonally right to rejoin the footpath. Go through a kissing gate and straight ahead up a field to a further kissing gate into a wood. As you enter the wood the path forks, take the right fork for a short distance to emerge at a stables and paddock. Follow the footpath directly across fields to High Road. Turn right.

7. Just after passing a house 'Marksland' cross over and turn left onto a bridleway to Park Farm. Where the track turns towards farm buildings cross a stile and go diagonally left across a field to a further stile. Follow the footpath round the edge of Upper Gatton wood, crossing two stiles, to the field where you retrace your steps to Fanny's Farm.

---

8. Woldingham & Limpsfield

Route: This is a beautiful but strenuous walk, one for the seasoned rambler. The route follows the steep, chalk paths (slippery in wet weather) of the North Downs Way and the Vanguard Way across scenic downland and through fine beech woodland. There are superb views at all stages: even the thunderous traffic on the M25 in the valley below fails to detract from the amazing view across the Weald from Oxted Downs.

Teashop: The Conservatory Coffee Shop, adjacent to Knight's Garden Centre, is an extension of a lovely (private) house set in a beautiful garden. From the conservatory and an attractive patio there is a superb view across the downland. The menu offers a good selection of sandwiches, baked potatoes and homemade quiches, cakes and scones. Set lunches are served between 12.00noon-2.30pm. It is open daily from 9.30am-4.30pm. Closed Christmas and New Year. Tel: 01883 652712.

Distance: 9 miles or 5¼ miles (omit instructions 4 & 5).

How to get there: Leave the M25 at junction 6. Follow the A22 for 2½ miles to Wapses Lodge Roundabout. Turn right to Woldingham.

Public transport: Trains: Connex South Central.

Start: GR 359564. Woldingham Road car park.

Maps: Landranger 187, Pathfinder 1207 & 1208, Explorer 146 & 147.

---

1. From the car park return to the road and turn right, pass the railway station and keep forward along Church Road. Where the road turns right at a 'No Through Road' sign, continue ahead on a gravel lane. Pass Church Farm and a few houses then, at the far end of the first field, turn left over a stile into the field and climb alongside a fence to a stile. From the stile, climb 104 shallow steps to a quiet country road. Turn right along the road for a quarter of a mile to a main road. Turn right for 30 metres then keep forward along Upper Court Road. Where the road starts to curve right at a house 'Sylvan Mount' turn left onto a narrow chalk path and descend steeply to a lane.

2. Cross diagonally right into Southview Road, an unmade road.

Just beyond a white house on the left, as the road climbs to the right, bear left on a narrow path. The path gently climbs up the valley, with lovely views left across the rolling downland; it continues, via a stile, along the valley bottom and then, from a further stile, it climbs long and steep to a stile into a field. Follow a left-hand boundary of fine larch and beech and turn left to a road. Cross over into a parking area, walk through to the far side and join a fenced path alongside a quarry. The path soon returns to the road. Turn right for 40 metres to a junction.

3. Turn right towards Oxted: the road is narrow and busy, so take care. After 80 metres turn left and descend to a stile. Cross onto Oxted Downs (NT) and descend a steep chalk path. Just as you become convinced that we must be taking you straight to the motorway, a waymarked junction is reached. For 9 mile walkers, this junction is returned to later in the walk.

Shortened Version: *Continue descending and pick up the instructions from 'Here turn left and descend...' in paragraph 6.*

4. Turn left onto the North Downs Way (NDW) and follow the path along the bottom of the down. (Although now walking parallel to the motorway with its constant roar of non-stop traffic, there are superb views to enjoy, across the Weald and to the South Downs on the horizon.) Turn right over a stile and descend to a stile into a very large open field. Follow an undulating path along the top of this field and a further field. Cross a stile and go down seven steps to a chalk track. Turn right and descend to a gate by an attractive farmhouse. Pass through the gate and continue to the entrance of Titsey Foundation Walk and Park. Here keep forward on a bridleway through light woodland. After half a mile the bridleway passes under the motorway then continues to the main road. Turn right along the road; it is very busy, so take care. After 260 metres, at the 30 mile an hour signs, bear left on a footpath to a clearing. Cross diagonally left to a path adjacent to a market garden. The path leads to Limpsfield Cemetery thence to St Peter's Church. Leave via the Lychgate and turn left along High Street.

St Peter's Church is a Wealden building much altered over the centuries. An unusual surviving relic in the chancel is the remains of an oven once

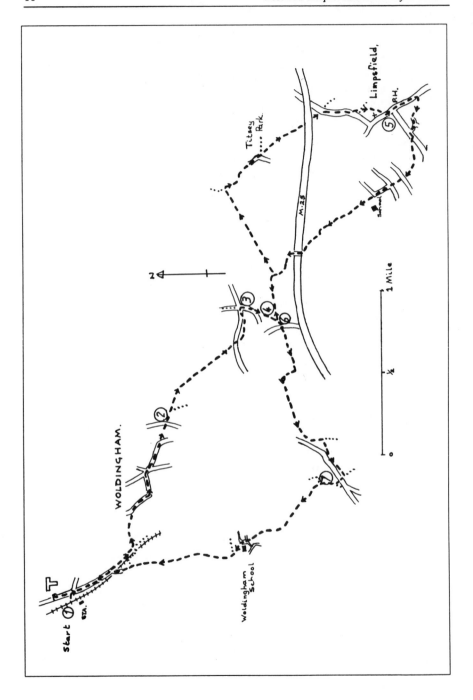

used for baking communion bread. The 14th-century lychgate is possibly the only survivor of its kind in Surrey. In the cemetery is the grave of the composer Delius. Having lived in France for more than 30 years, Delius died in 1934 and was buried there. In 1935, respecting his last wishes, his remains were transferred to Limpsfield. Sir Thomas Beecham, a great admirer of Delius, led a torchlight service at his re-burial. Beecham's grave is near that of Delius in what has become, over the years, a Musician's Corner.

Limpsfield is set on the Wealden ridge near the Kent border. Its long history is reflected in the many old picturesque houses in the High Street. On the corner with Detillens Lane is a terrace of 15th-century timber-framed cottages: across the road, almost hidden in the trees, is a shed which was once the privy for these cottages. Opposite the Bull Inn is Detillens, a rare 15th-century hall-house with an early 18th-century facade: it is a fine example of property owned by Surrey yeomen – freeholders who farmed their own land. Further along the High Street is 12th-century Old Court Cottage, once the home of the abbott of Battle who held manorial court there. Opposite the Post Office two attractive buildings complete the picturesque scene; a long single storey building with herringbone brickwork and decorated barge-board, built in 1927 and the 18th-century timber-framed and tile-hung Rosewell Cottage.

5. Pass Detillens Lane and the cottages on its corner and walk up the High Street as far as the Post Office. Here turn right along Priest Hill. Keep forward at a waymarked post then pass through a kissing gate into a housing development. Follow the road down and through the development to Detillens Lane. Turn left for 50 metres then turn right, between houses, to a stile into a meadow. Bear left across the meadow. Pass through a horse barrier and over a footbridge. Keep alongside a field, with a view of the church tower on the right, and emerge at a road. Cross over and continue between houses to a further road. Cross diagonally right into Park Road. Where the road turns right, keep forward on a fenced path alongside a school. Cross a stile into a large open field. Follow the left-hand hedgerow up the field, with lovely views ahead to Oxted Downs and the undulating fields walked through earlier. The path leads to a footbridge over the motorway;

Detillens Cottages, Limpsfield

cross this and turn left along a grassy path. Cross a stile into the (undulating) field and follow the left-hand hedgerow up to the stile on the left. Over the stile retrace the NDW along the bottom of Oxted Downs to the waymarked junction used earlier in the walk.

6. Here turn left and descend steeply to a stile and a path to a road. Turn right for 40 metres then left, alongside a house, to a stile and a wide grassy path between fences. Follow a quarry boundary for half a mile: although the quarry is not too obvious – the 'Danger' notices are! Turn right with the fence and climb to a kissing gate: from the gate climb steeply to an Oxted Downs (NT) sign. Turn left and follow the undulating NDW across the Down and through diverse woodland for a quarter of a mile to a stile. Turn right over the stile and climb 112 steps. On the numerous stops en route look back to the Weald, the motorway and the railway line emerging from its tunnel under the Downs. At the top of the steps turn left, ignore steps on the right to the road and continue on the NDW; now on a more level path and soon passing a welcome seat. Turn right at a junction (NDW) and climb almost to the road. Do not go to the road, instead turn left for a further 300 metres through woodland then meet the road. Here leave the NDW, cross the road and pass through a narrow barrier into woodland.

Marden Park Wood (154 acres) was open landscape until purchased by Sir Robert Clayton, Lord Mayor of London (1679-1680) who built his estate here and planted several plantations. The orchestral conductor, Sir Adrian Boult, who subsequently sold it to the Forestry Commission, owned Great Church Wood (12 acres). Today the woods are managed by the Woodland Trust and are designated Areas of Outstanding Natural Beauty.

7. Follow a narrow footpath to a fork, keep right and join a permissive bridleway. Turn right along the bridleway - two metres ahead the path is signed Woldingham Country Walk (these WCW signs eventually lead back to the car park). Where the permissive bridleway turns away sharp right, follow the WCW as it bears left on a broad footpath. On reaching a fork at a clearing, fork left on

the WCW. The path gently descends and wends its way through the wood with WCW waymarks en route. Emerge from the wood at a stile into a meadow. Turn right on a gently descending curving path, with a splendid view across the downland and to Woldingham Convent School. Leave the meadow via a stile to a lane (signed Woldingham Station 1½ miles). Keep forward and, as the lane turns right, bear left along a track. Climb gently through woodland, ignoring a path right to South Hawke, then gently descend for some time between fields to Marden Park Farm, now converted into apartments. From the farm, continue along the road to a junction. Turn left to return to the car park. The teashop is a further 300 metres beyond the car park.

9. Lingfield

Route:	This is an easy flat walk mainly over open farmland. There are lovely views at various points; the picturesque old town is a delight to explore.
Teashop:	Joyce's with Best Wishes is a delightful combination of tea shop and speciality greetings card shop. It has four cosy dining rooms and a lovely secluded garden. The service is friendly; the lunches and cakes, all home-made, are excellent. Open Monday – Saturday 9.00am – 5.30pm. Tel: 01342 832428
Distance:	5 miles.
How to get there:	From East Grinstead follow the A22 to the B2028. Turn right to Lingfield.
Public Transport:	Bus services: Arriva. Trains: Connex South Central.
Start:	GR 386435. Free public car park at the corner of Plaistow Street and High Street.
Maps:	Landranger 187, Pathfinder 1227 TQ24/34, Explorer 146

Lingfield village has developed between two main points. At one end is St Peter's Cross and Gun Pond and at the other, forming one of the most attractive architectural corners in Surrey, is the large parish church and a group of buildings dating from the 15th century.

St Peter's Cross was built in 1473 to mark the boundary between two manors. The cage, added in 1773 as a prison, was last used in 1882. On one occasion it housed as many as eleven poachers. The Lingfield oak is thought to be about 400 years old, despite the hollow centre its abundance of summer greenery proves it is still very healthy.

1. From the car park return to the main road. Cross at St Peter's Cross and walk down Vicarage Road. Just before the road curves to the right turn left onto a footpath. Where the footpath becomes a driveway take the lower footpath on the right. Cross a stile and continue ahead through three fields to a car park and road. Cross

'The Cage' at Lingfield

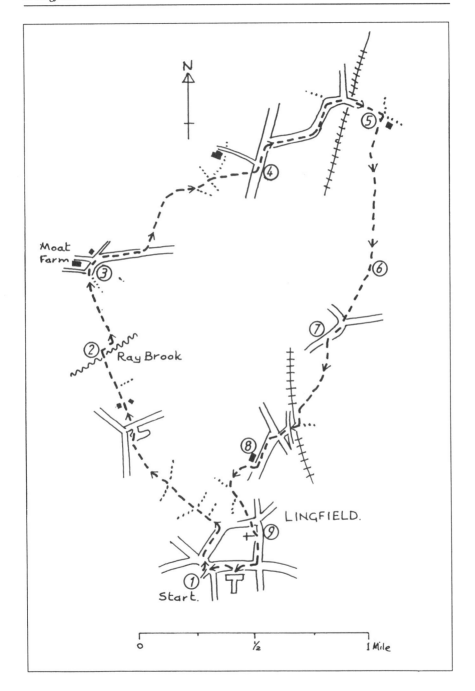

to a footpath opposite; where the path becomes a private drive turn down a narrow footpath between two houses. Ignoring a stile on the right, cross the stile ahead into a field and follow the path round to a footbridge over Ray Brook.

2. Turn right and in a few metres go through a gate, over a footbridge and follow the path through to cross a stile into a field. Continue ahead towards a large single oak and two large houses in the background. Turn towards the large cream house and cross two stiles to join the road at Moat Farm.

3. Turn right to a house named The Barn. Turn right along a wide track to a stile on the left. Cross into a field and follow the path up, keeping to the hedge on the left. At the second field bear slightly right to a signpost. Turn right along the field edge to cross a stile. Continue along the field to a waymarked post and stile into an orchard. Continue alongside the orchard to a stile and continue ahead through a field and into woodland. Turn left passing a small marker post and follow the path to a third post. Turn right down a short path and cross a stile. Cross a field to a stile on the right of a timber-framed house.

4. Turn left along Crowhurst Road then right into Pikes Lane. This is a long, quite busy winding road but it goes past two interesting houses, Oast House and Pikes Farm, and there are open views on the left. Leave the road where it turns left and turn right to cross the railway. Here the road becomes more of a country lane.

5. Just before reaching farm buildings cross two stiles on the right leading into a large field. Head for a large oak at the top of the field and cross a stile behind it. Follow alongside a small wood, cross a stile and head for three oak trees in the far hedgerow where there is a stile.

From this point, on a clear day, four churches are visible, East Grinstead, Lingfield, The Mormon Temple and Crowhurst. The hedgerow is a crossing point of the Greenwich Meridian, in crossing the stile you have crossed from the Eastern to the Western Hemisphere.

6. Turn right down a field to a signpost. Turn slightly left to cross two fields. Turn right and follow two more fields down to the junction of Bowerland Lane and Haxted Road.

7. This is a very dangerous corner so take great care when turning right into Haxted Road. Just over the bridge turn left onto a footpath then diagonally right across two fields to a gate post. Cross the top of the field to a stile in the right-hand corner. Cross a track into a field and follow the footpath through a gate. Keep to the field edge on the right and go through a white gate on the right to cross the railway. Continue ahead through a small development then turn left into Saxbys Lane.

8. At the Fire Station turn right and follow the footpath through a gate and immediately left to cross a field then left again to the recreation ground. Cross diagonally right then take the footpath ahead to the church.

The Guest House, a beautiful 15th century timber-framed building, once housed visitors in the days when the church had its own college. Now converted to Lingfield library it has retained many original features including a minstrel's gallery: if open it is well worth a visit.

Although dating from the 12th century, the church of St Peter and St Paul was largely re-built in 1431. The church, almost large enough to be a city church, contains Surrey's only medieval choir stall and the finest set of brasses to be found in the county. It also houses the tombs of the Cobham family who were responsible for the re-building of the church.

The group of buildings in the old town were built as houses, shops and an inn. Pollard House and Cottage, the oldest house in the group, is a fine example of a Wealden house. The projecting wing dates from about 1500 and is a rare example of a medieval shop.

9. Leave the church by the double gates to walk through the old town. Turn right along the main road to the tea shop. Continue along the road to return to the car park.

10. Sidney Wood & Alfold

Route: The route follows woodland bridleways, field paths and a disused canal. As some sections of the bridleways can be very muddy, the walk is easier to do in dry weather. However, the wood is most beautiful in springtime when there is a profusion of wood anemones, primroses, celandine and bluebells.

Teashop: Springbok Tea Room is an extension of the farm shop. It sells sausage rolls, pasties, toasted teacakes, biscuits, ice-creams and hot and cold drinks. Muddy boots are no problem here, the loo is outside and there are picnic tables in a pleasant courtyard. It is open from 10.30am-5.00pm. February-October daily. November-January, Saturday and Sunday only. Tel: 01403 752555.

Distance: 4¾ miles.

How to get there: From the A281 at Alfold Crossways take the Dunsfold road. The car park is 1¼ miles on the left.

Public transport: Bus service: Tillingbourne.

Start: GR 027352. Sidney Wood Forestry Commission car park.

Maps: Landranger 186, Pathfinder TQ03/13, Explorer 134.

1. The walk begins at the Forestry Commission information board, which explains the origin of the name Sidney Wood. Facing the notice board, turn right to the third parking bay and pass between two barrier posts onto an indistinct grassy path. Follow the path round to the right and soon reach a junction. Turn left along a wide bridleway: although not signed this is the Wey South Path, it is extremely muddy after rain. The path soon descends to a lane; cross over and continue on the Wey South Path, now signed and with a much firmer surface. Pass an entrance to Fir Tree Copse on the right and continue to a fork. Fork right: in late April the bluebells, primroses, wood anemones and violets along this path are quite spellbinding. Shortly pass by a gate, cross the disused Wey & Arun Junction Canal and keep forward alongside a pine plantation on the left.

The Wey & Arun Junction Canal opened in 1816 and formed an 18½ mile link between the Thames at Weybridge and the River Arun at Newbridge; it was the only inland water link between the Thames and the English Channel. From the coast came seaweed, grain, coal and a variety of food and merchandise. Barges returned with bark, timber, flour and goods made by the rural industries. Locally chalk, clay, sand and gravel were transported between the pits and villages. The route, however, was never used to capacity. With the opening of the Guildford-Horsham Railway in 1865 it fell into decline and finally closed in 1871. In 1970, the Wey & Arun Canal Trust began restoration of various sections of the derelict canal.

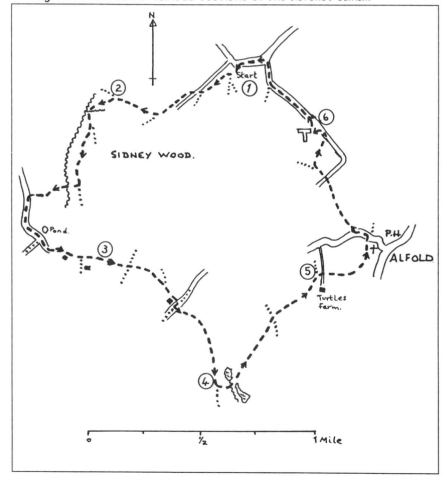

2. Reach a waymarked post at the end of the plantation and turn left. The path bears right and soon descends to a stream on the right. Keep parallel to the stream for 30 metres then turn right onto a narrow path which bears left and gently undulates through the basin of the wood (bluebells and celandine here). In approximately a quarter of a mile the path reaches a footbridge over the stream. Turn right over the footbridge for a short steep climb, turn right to a farm and join a track to a road. Turn left along the road; there is no pavement so take care. The road descends to a gravel bridleway on the right; ignore this and continue ahead, now ascending and soon passing Lock House Lodge and Sydney Court (once Old Lock House).

In the mid-nineteenth century these houses, then adjacent to Lock XV, were the main offices and workshop for the Canal Company. The lodge was the home of John Cole and his family who lived there for over 30 years carrying out repairs, constructing lock-gates and building boats.

3. On reaching Sidney Wood follow the main path straight through the wood, keeping forward at a wide track. In about a quarter of a mile pass through a gate and follow a track to a road. Turn right for 30 metres then left onto a towpath to follow the disused canal for almost half a mile; watch for spotted orchid as you walk.

4. On reaching a waymarked signpost turn left across the canal (a future proposal is to flood the canal and put a footbridge here). Cross a stile and keep forward, passing a small fishing lake on the left. Cross a footbridge, pass through a gate ahead and keep forward to a stile into a field. Cross the field to a stile, on the right of woodland, into another field. Follow the left-hand boundary to two gates, ignore the gate on the left and go through the gate ahead. Bear left across the field to a farm track and a gate into yet another field. Cross diagonally to a stile and footbridge. Keep forward alongside a fence on the right to a stile.

5. Turn right over the stile then cross two private driveways to a stile into a field. Follow the right-hand boundary, descending to a stream and two stiles. Over the stiles go straight across the next two fields, gently climbing to a stile and a kissing gate into a cemetery. Cross to a further kissing gate and continue to a road. Turn

left for 100 metres then turn right onto a narrow path. Keep forward over a stile then reach a stile into a field. Follow the left-hand boundary to a footbridge and stile into a field. Bear right across the field to a stile to a road. Cross straight over to a stile and planked footbridge into a field. Cross diagonally right to a further planked footbridge and stile to the road. Turn left to the teaoom.

The tearoom and farmshop is the fundraising arm of the Merchant Seamen's War Memorial Society. The estate was purchased when a gift of £200,000 was given by the people of South Africa as a mark of respect to seamen who lost their lives in the Second World War. Over the next 48 years, some 1500 disabled seafarers were retrained on the estate as farm workers, market gardeners and maintenance men. Today the main house and the bungalows provide accommodation and social activites for retired and disabled ex-merchant seamen.

The Victorian walled garden has been worked continuously for over 100 years. It produces flowers and vegetables for the shop and main house and is used to train ex-merchant seamen into a new career as gardeners.

'Swan Lake' – see point 4 on this walk

6. From the tea room turn left and follow the road round to the right, passing a lake and the Merchant Seamen memorial anchor. Turn right at farm buildings and continue to the main road. Turn left for 250 metres then left into the car park.

11. Mytchett and the Basingstoke Canal

Route: An easy walk through varied terrain, much of which is owned by the Ministry of Defence. The route starts on woodland paths, undulates across heathland and ends along an attractive 2¾-mile stretch of Basingstoke Canal towpath.

Teashop: The Canal Tea Room is in a conservatory overlooking the canal. On a sunny day outside seating on a pleasant patio will appeal. The menu offers homemade cakes and scones, a good selection of light lunches plus various ice-creams and cold drinks. It is open Easter-September, Tuesday-Friday 10.30am-5.30pm; Saturday, Sunday and Bank Holiday Mondays 10.00am-6.30pm. Winter, open weekends only, 11.00am-5.00pm. Tel: 01252 524217.

Distance: 5¾ miles or 3¼ miles (omit instructions 4 & 5).

How to get there: The Visitor Centre is on Mytchett Place Road off the A321 Ash to Frimley Road.

Public transport: Bus services: Stagecoach Hants & Surrey, Tillingbourne.

Start: GR 893550. Basingstoke Canal Visitor Centre car park.

Maps: Landranger 186, Pathfinder 1205 SU85/95, Explorer 145.

Basingstoke Canal opened in 1794 to carry flour, malt and timber to London and coal, groceries and china back to Hampshire. Despite numerous attempts to maintain its commercial viability the canal was never very successful. There was strong competition from road, sea and rail, but the main cause of its lack of success was the failure to extend the canal beyond Basingstoke. It flourished once more in the 1850s when used for transporting materials for the construction of Aldershot Camp and again during World War I when stores and munitions were carried. However commercial traffic continued to decrease and the canal finally closed in 1949, from which time it lay neglected and derelict.

The Visitor Centre, Basingstoke Canal

In 1974 the Hampshire Canal Society with Hampshire and Surrey Councils and hundreds of enthusiastic volunteers started restoration work. The canal was dredged, the towpath reinstated and many bridges and locks rebuilt. On one weekend in October 1977 over 600 workers took part in 'Deepcut Dig'. Today the Deepcut flight of 14 locks raises the water level by 29 metres (94 feet). The canal is now a popular leisure attraction and there is a wonderful 33½-mile towpath trail from Penny Bridge to its junction with the River Wey at Woodham. The Visitor Centre contains interesting information on the history of the canal and a working model of a lock; it also offers excellent camping facilities in nearby fields.

1. From the car park return to the road. Turn left then immediately left again along a broad track. Turn right through a barrier gate for 12 metres then turn left onto a woodland path. On reaching a fork, bear right for 40 metres then fork left. Pass a path on the right and continue to a junction of five paths.

2. Here turn left along the perimeter of the wood. Pass between two small barrier posts, where a sign reads 'Out of Bounds to

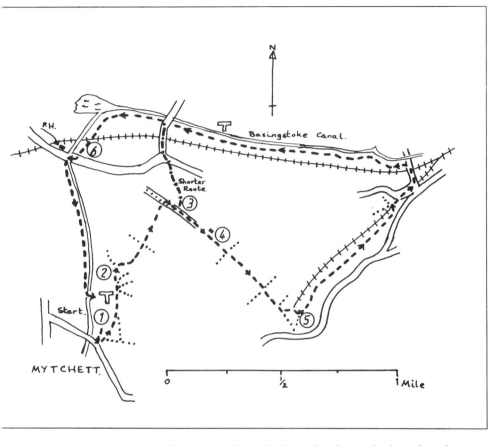

Troops'and gradually descend to a fork. Take the right-hand path and gently ascend, first to the right then left. Keep ahead at a crossing path with overhead electrical cables. The path climbs past a house 'Four Winds' and continues to a road. Turn right along the road and soon pass a telecommunication mast on the left.

3. **Shortened Version:** *Thirty metres beyond the mast, at an electricity pole, turn left between two concrete posts. The path passes between conifers and descends, soon past open fields on the left, to emerge at the road (B3012). Cross directly over into Deepcut Bridge Road. Continue along the road until reaching Deepcut Bridge. Descend the steps at the side of the bridge and turn left along the*

towpath. Follow the walk instructions from the beginning of paragragh 6.

4. At a house 'Rangelands' the road degenerates into a track. Continue along this track for three-quarters of a mile until reaching a barriered path on the left with a 'No Parking, Emergency Access' sign. Ten metres beyond the sign turn left over the bank for 12 metres then turn right. The path sweeps round an S-Bend and joins a path from the right.

5. Here turn left. From this point on ignore all paths off on the right and continue for three-quarters of a mile across undulating heathland to a tunnel. En route, negotiate two short steep descents, pass Longdown Hill on the right then fork left onto a narrow path alongside the railway track. Turn left under the tunnel then right onto a wide path. Reach a barrier gate to a road. Taking care, turn right and cross over to a lane on the left. The lane ascends to a railway bridge and a canal bridge (Curzon Bridges). Turn left and descend to the towpath.

This first section of the canal is flanked by deciduous woodland and whatever the time of year there should always be something of interest to enjoy. In early spring when the Malus (Siberian crab) was at its prettiest and birds in full song we were fortunate to spy a handsome yellowhammer. Watch out for tufted duck (snowy-white flanks and blue beak) among diverse water birds. From Deepcut Bridge, the scenery changes a little: attractive gardens lead down to the canal; there is an extremely long bank of wild rhododendrons – a picture in late spring – and finally Wharfenden Lake is passed.

6. Leave the towpath at a lane to join the main road. Turn right over the canal bridge (Guildford Road Bridge) and cross over to the south towpath. The canal is now flanked by woodland on the left and Frimley Park to the right. The park has a small-gauge railway with some beautiful little steam trains; it runs on the first Sunday in the month March-November plus Bank Holidays and occasional special trips. On reaching the swingbridge, cross the canal to the Visitor Centre and the tearoom.

12. The Devil's Punch Bowl, Gibbet Hill and Hindhead Common

Route: This short but energetic walk along dry sandy tracks discovers the 'ups and downs' of the Devil's Punchbowl and takes in the glorious views from Sugar Loaf Hill and Gibbet Hill.

Teashop: The National Trust's Devil's Punch Bowl Café, on the A3, is situated just 50 metres from the stunning scenery of Surrey's most unusual natural landscape. The café is open daily from 8.00am to 5.00pm but closed 25 and 26 December and 1 January. A selection of homemade hot and cold meals is available plus homemade cakes and scones. There is seating outside and a picnic area nearby. Tel: 01428 608771. Car park charges will apply.

Distance: 4¼ miles.

How to get there: Hindhead is on the A3 approximately 13 miles south of Guildford.

Public Transport: Bus services: Stagecoach Coachline.

Start: GR 891357. The Punchbowl/Hillcrest Café car park close to the Hindhead traffic lights at the A3/A287 crossing.

Maps: Landranger 186, Pathfinder 1245 SU83/93, Explorer 133

Hindhead Common owned by the National Trust (NT) comprises 1400 acres of valuable heathland which supports a great diversity of flora and fauna. Pine, birch and bracken have become invasive over the years and there is danger of this valuable habitat being lost. In order to regenerate the growth of heather and encourage more habitation, the NT are currently grazing Highland cattle, Exmoor and New Forest ponies in selected areas of the common.

The Devil's Punch Bowl, the most dominant feature of the common, is one of the largest spring-eroded valleys in Europe. This natural chasm has formed over thousands of years by a series of springs cutting through and eroding the sandy beds of the Lower Greensand.

Keeper's Cottage and 'The Punch Bowl'

Local folklore states that the Devil, living at Devil's Jumps near Churt, was constantly in battle with Thor, the God of Thunder, who lived at Thor's-Lie (Thursley). One day the Devil scooped a handful of earth and hurled it at Thor: the resulting depression became forever linked with the Devil. It is said the Punch Bowl is so named because mist lying in the bowl rises and appears to flow over the rim of the bowl as if it were boiling.

1. From the café side of the car park take a path on the left of the NT sign. Go down some wide steps and turn left to Highcombe Edge. Follow this wide pleasant track for approximately half a mile to a junction.

2. Take a broad track on the right of the drive to Broom Acres, soon passing a seat and a viewpoint on the right. Just beyond a seat on the left, at a fork, bear right then turn immediately right onto a path which ends at a viewpoint and the Robertson Memorial.

The memorial commemorates the gift of Highcombe Edge and Highcombe

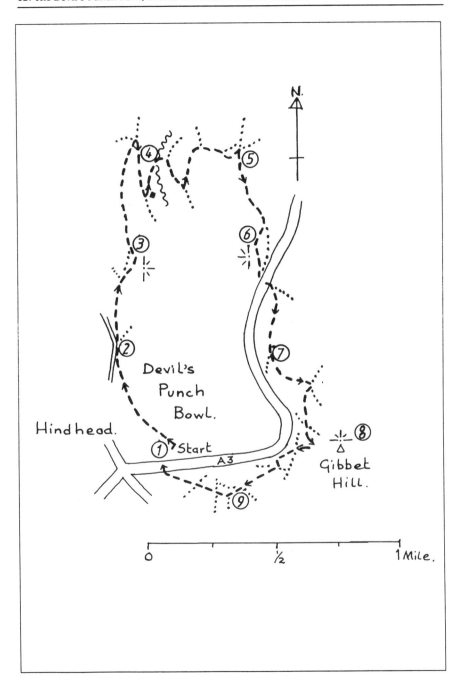

Copse to the NT by W A Robertson in memory of his two brothers killed in the Great War – a generous and apt way of keeping alive the memory of those who fought for freedom.

3. Continue past the memorial to return to the main track and turn right: the track gradually descends for approximately half a mile to a crossing path. Turn right to continue descending. On reaching an open field turn left, in front of a gate, onto a track which descends past Keepers Cottage, a pretty half-timbered building, to a footbridge at Highcombe Bottom. This pretty valley with its trickling stream is a haven of tranquillity – even the traffic on the A3 above can hardly be heard.

4. Over the footbridge the track ascends to a gate. Go through the gate and turn right. At a junction turn left (seat and beautiful viewpoint on the right). Just after the track curves right keep ahead at a crossing path and continue to a fork.

5. Follow the path on the right to a way-marked post at a crossing path. Turn right onto the Greensand Way; the track gradually climbs to superb views (there is a seat on the right almost hidden behind the shrubs). Continue along the track and as it descends watch for a narrow path on the right just beyond some barrier stumps.

6. Follow this path for a very short climb to Sugar Loaf Hill from where there are superb panoramic views across the Punch Bowl. Cross the hill and descend a track to go through a gate and continue to the A3. Taking great care, cross the A3 diagonally left to a signpost. After 10 metres take a right fork; the path rises and falls then levels out.

7. After approximately a quarter of a mile, where the path divides, keep to the lower left path; the path descends and eventually curves right to immediately meet a crossing path. Turn right for a steep climb. Ignore a minor fork to the right and shortly cross a bridleway and go through a horse barrier for a short climb to Gibbet Hill (892ft/272m).

An OS trig point identifies the spectacular views across the Weald and the Surrey hills. Gibbet Cross marks the spot where three sailors were hanged in 1786 for the 'barbarous' murder of an unknown sailor. The Latin inscription translates as "After death, safety; In death, peace; In life, hope; After darkness, light". The Sailor's Stone, a memorial on the old Portsmouth Road, was erected soon after the murder.

8. With the OS trig point behind, follow a wide grassy path to a parking area and take a gravel track on the right. The track turns left and in approximately 100 metres passes the Sailor's stone on the right. Four metres beyond the stone turn left onto a narrow rough path. After approximately 12 metres turn right onto a footpath. Continue ahead at a crossing path (marker post here) and soon pass through a clearing onto a wide track.

9. As the track curves right take the second of two paths on the left. After 25 metres fork right onto a grassy path. Continue ahead at each of two crossing paths. Keep right at a fork on the left. At a T-junction turn left then right at a NT workshop. Carefully cross the A3 to the car park and café.

13. Haslemere and South Park Moat

Route: An easy, almost level walk through fields and woodland. It is recommended for a summer walk as the fields are very muddy in winter. The medieval moat is an interesting and pretty spot for a rest.

Teashop: Darnley's café offers friendly service, homemade cakes, scones and light lunches. The High Street takes on a continental air in fine weather when tables are set on the wide pavement area outside the café. Open Friday to Saturday 9.30am – 5.00pm. Sunday 10.00am – 5.00pm. Tel: 01428 643048

Distance: 5¼ miles.

How to get there: Haslemere is on the A286 approximately 9 miles south of Godalming.

Public Transport: Bus services: Stagecoach Coastline. Trains: South West Trains.

Start: GR 904329. Haslemere town car park.

Maps: Landranger 186, Pathfinder 1245 SU 83/93, Explorer 133

Standing guard at the southern end of the High Street is the old Town Hall, first built in the 1500s as a Market Hall. The earliest reference to Haslemere is in 1221 when it was included in the Manor of Godalming. In 1596 Queen Elizabeth I granted 'for the relief of the town and its poor inhabitants', a Charter of a Market and two Fairs. The custom of holding a Charter Fair was revived in 1982: parades, maypole dancing and fancy dress competitions are among the many attractions of this popular event, held biannually on the first Bank Holiday in May.

Further along is the Educational Museum. The museum was founded in 1888 by Dr Jonathan Hutchinson at his residence 'Inval' where it started life in two large barns. Doctor Hutchinson gave weekly lectures and demonstrations and whenever possible live specimens of animal and plant life were exhibited. His progressive methods became an example for small museums throughout the world. The museum, which today plays a significant role within the community, was finally transferred to the High Street in 1925.

The town's one note of infamy is that the first killing of a policeman in Surrey happened in Haslemere. In 1855, navvies working on the new railway marched to the prison cell in the Market Hall to rescue a fellow worker imprisoned for drunkenness. During the ensuing battle a police inspector was fatally injured. Two plaques on the wall of the Town Hall commemorate both this event and the name of Robert Hunter, a co-founder of the National Trust, who lived in Haslemere.

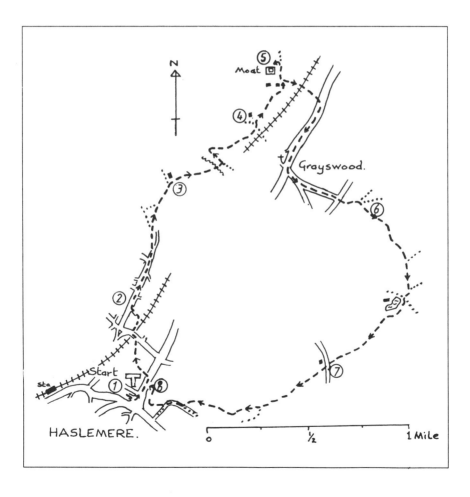

1. From the town car park turn left up High Street. 25 metres beyond the Georgian Hotel turn left along a footpath between houses. (A plaque on the wall denotes the start of the Greensand Way.) Turn left at the road, cross the railway bridge and turn immediately right along the footpath by the railway.

2. On reaching the recreation ground turn right to the end of the road. Continue ahead towards a wood. 10 metres beyond a 'Ramp Ahead' sign take a footpath on the left: this path, which can be very muddy in winter, leads through the wood and eventually passes through an iron gate. Follow the path through a further gate by a three-way signpost.

3. Walk round Keffolds Farmhouse and go through a field gate on the right. The lovely view from here is towards the surrounding Greensand hills. Follow the direction of a yellow waymark across the field and down a tree-lined sunken path. Over a stile the path follows a wired fence on the left, drops down to cross a stream, then ascends. Cross a stile on the left of a gate marked Private. Bear slightly left across a field to another stile. Turn right along a farm track.

4. On reaching a three-way junction at the drive to Damson Cottage cross to a stile on the right and follow a narrow footpath through woodland: in 60 metres pass through an iron kissing gate. Cross a stream then head uphill: as the field levels out turn right by three oak trees and follow a farm fence on the left to a lane. Turn left for 30 metres then right onto the track to South Park Moat.

   In 1991 this site was donated to, and restored by, the Surrey Archaeological Society. Although the moat's history is uncertain, it is probable that a manor house existed here early in the 14th century. Artifacts discovered suggest there was a pre-moat settlement nearby and that human life existed around the moat from much earlier times. Further information is available from the Society and Haslemere Museum.

5. From the moat return to the lane, turn left and walk down to the main road. Turn right to Grayswood church (there is a large unusual memorial tablet by the church gate). Just beyond the church cross into Lower Road. Bear left at the first fork. On reach-

ing Prestwick Lane cross over to a bridleway: the track passes Southern Water Services on the left and continues to a gate.

6. Go through the gate onto a fenced footpath. At the end of the fence bear right through a gap and continue alongside a wire fence on the left. Go through a gate, bear diagonally left across a field then turn right along the fence-line. Continue ahead across the next field. Go through a gateway and turn immediately right at a two-way signpost. Turn left at a lane, passing Imbham's lake on the right then farm buildings on the left. Continue along the lane until reaching the junction with Holdfast Lane.

7. Cross over and follow a footpath by Holdfast Cottage. Cross a stile and turn right onto a track. Go through a gate at a National Trust sign to Swan Barn Farm. Keeping to the footpath, with trees on the right, cross three fields via footbridges then enter Witley Copse (NT). The footpath leads through the copse, following a fence on the right, to a footbridge. Over the footbridge the path curves left. Where the path sweeps right uphill, take the left fork

View from Town Well

downhill to cross a footbridge. Bear diagonally right across a field (often quite muddy) then turn right onto a broad track. Where the track curves left, turn right through a barrier. Cross a field diagonally left to a gate. Turn right to Haslemere Town Well.

From medieval times until the late 19th century this well was one of the main sources of water for the town. Haslemere's last public water carrier Hannah Oakford, who died in 1898, charged 1½d (old pence) per bucket to deliver water to houses in the town.

8. Turn left to the High Street then left to Darnleys' café. Continue along the High Street to the car park.

14. Petworth Park & Lodsworth

Route: This is a beautiful walk. The route leads across the rolling downland of Petworth Park, through woodland, beautiful with spring bluebells, and through three lovely Sussex villages. There are magnificent views to the South Downs and north to Blackdown at all stages.

Teashop: Lombard's Café bar, on the corner of Market Square, offers a warm welcome and friendly service. An extensive home cooked menu ranges from toasted teacakes, through a fine choice of lunches and teas, to candle-lit suppers. There is a mouth-watering selection of homemade cakes and scones – we can certainly recommend the dark chocolate cake! The café is open daily (except Christmas period) Tuesday to Saturday from 10.00am to 9.00pm. Sunday and Monday from 10.00am to 5.00pm. Tel: 01798 344264

Distance: 8½ miles.

How to get there: Petworth is 6 miles east of Midhurst at the junction of the A272/A283/A285.

Public transport: Bus service: Stagecoach Coastline.

Start: GR 976216. Petworth town car park (free).

Maps: Landranger 197, Pathfinder 1266 SU82/92, Explorer 133.

Petworth is a compact town set high on a sandstone ridge. It was once a centre for local iron working; Petworth marble was quarried in its vicinity and between the 14th and 16th centuries its wealth was acquired through the cloth-weaving industry. The town is dominated by the enormous wall of Petworth House and sits at the junction of three main roads. It is only by parking the car and exploring on foot that the beauty of its squares and narrow streets and its old attractive buildings and antique shops can be fully enjoyed.

Petworth – Peteorde in the Domesday Book – has changed little over the centuries. Market Square was a market place and the setting for street fairs for over 700 years: a street fair is still held annually in

November. In a corner of the square, a graceful wisteria-covered building with 'stopped' windows shows evidence of the Window Tax of 1762. Picturesque, cobbled Lombard Street, with iron-work-framed courtyards, has always been a busy shopping street: to-day, only the merchandise has changed. On one wall, a bull's head in blue and white tiles indicates where once there was a slaughter-house and a butcher's shop. At the junction of Church Street and East Street a lamp standard of thin spiralling ironwork is a monu-ment to Lord Leconfield who provided the town with gas lighting.

Petworth House, dating from the 14th century, stands in 700 acres of magnificent parkland protected by a wall over 13 miles long. The 6th Duke of Somerset rebuilt the elegant house, 97 metres (320 ft) long and only two rooms wide, in the French style in 1688. Now in the care of the National Trust it houses the Trust's finest collection of paintings with works by Blake, Rembrandt, Reynolds and Van Dyck; with a special room for Turner.

The famous Park, immortalized by paintings of Turner, is home to over 400 fallow deer. In 1754 under the direction of the Second Earl

Petworth Park

of Egremont the park was landscaped by Lancelot 'Capability' Brown. Groups of oak, beech and sweet chestnut were planted in vast sweeps of lawn and downland and, from a series of small ponds and marshland, the tranquil serpentine lake was created. A perfect example of Capability's artistic genius is the marvellous view from the top of the park, looking back through mature trees where deer quietly graze, across the lake to the west front of the house.

1. From the right-hand corner of the car park follow the footpath adjacent to the public toilets. At the road continue ahead through Golden Square and Market Square and along Lombard Street. At the main road turn right and follow the road round to the left: the pavement narrows on the bend so take great care. After 100 metres enter Petworth Park via its tradesman's entrance The Cowyard. Follow the path down, turn left through a tunnel and pass through the park gates. Bear left on a grassy path which curves right along the bottom of a hill towards the lake. Keep the lake on your left and follow the water's edge to a stone built boathouse. Pause on the patio for the beautiful view down the lake then continue left as the path traces a line of metal railings round the head of the lake.

2. As the end of the railings come into sight turn right along a wide grassy ascending path. Reach a junction and turn right onto a main gravel path. The path gently ascends and passes through a small copse of beech. From the beech it descends to a deer-fenced copse on the left: as the fence turns left go diagonally left across the parkland, immediately passing on the right of some ancient sweet chestnut and heading for the far corner of the fence. On reaching the corner keep the fence on your left and climb to a wire gate at the junction with the park wall. Through the gate continue alongside the wall, pass through a further gate and turn left to the road.

3. Turn right to walk through Upperton. (The road turns right, it leads straight through the village then out towards Lurgashall.) Pass a road junction to Pitshill and a bridleway on the left. Just beyond the brow of the hill, opposite a tower on the right, turn left

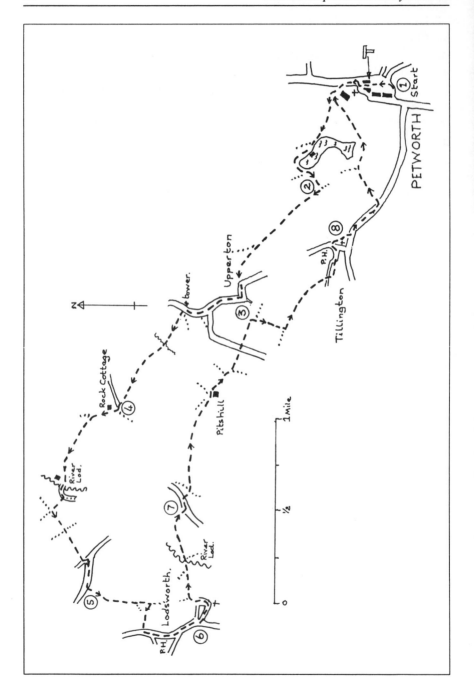

onto the right-hand of two paths and descend through a wood. At the bottom of the wood cross a small stream, ignore a raised path which goes left over a planked footbridge and within 50 metres cross another stream. Continue for almost half a mile then emerge from the wood onto a common and keep forward to a lane.

4. Turn left for 30 metres then turn right, past Rock Cottage and along a farm track. On reaching a three-way signpost turn left over a stile into a field. Follow the left-hand hedgerow down until it turns left then cross diagonally right to a gate on the left of an electricity pole with a transformer. Pass through the gate, cross to the left of a building ahead then go through a kissing gate and down a drive. Cross the River Lod, turn left for 45 metres then right over a stile into a field. Follow a left-hand hedgerow, passing under pylon cables, to a crossing path at the field corner. Cross the stile on the left and keep forward to pass under the cables again. Cross a drive onto a broad woodland path. Keep ahead at a crossing track and ignore all paths off; the path climbs steeply for the last 100 metres to a lane. Turn left to a road junction then right along a road ascending to Leggatt Hill Farm.

5. Turn left through the farm gate, pass the farmhouse, go through another gate and keep forward on a grassy track. The track soon turns right then left to a gate with a stile on the left. Cross the stile and keep along the top of a field to a stile into a wood. In 20 metres ignore a narrow path right and descend to a junction. Turn sharp right and leave the wood via a footbridge and stile into a field. Climb up the field to a stile to a road. Turn left to walk through Lodsworth, passing the Hollist Arms on the right.

6. Where the road curves right at 'Woodmancote', the home for twenty-one years of the artist E.H. Shepherd, turn left down a lane. Pass St Peter's Church on the right and continue down until reaching a cottage 'St Peter's Well'. Here, turn right onto a tiny green (the well is on the left side). Pass through a gate and in 45 metres turn right and descend between fencing to a gate and bridge across the River Lod. Twenty-five metres beyond the bridge, fork left and ascend through a wood. Join a path merging from the right for 15 metres then fork right. The path continues

climbing and soon curves right and skirts the wood. Cross a stile
and continue by a garden to a further stile to a lane. Turn left for
90 metres to a stile on the right.

7. Cross the stile and climb through woodland via a series of steps.
   Cross a stile and a sunken path and turn left along the higher
   path. The path climbs through a hanger with views left towards
   Blackdown. On the steady descent the path merges with a path
   from the left, keep right. On reaching a drive and the private garden of Pitshill Manor turn left. Ignore a drive left and continue to
   a cattle grid: fifteen metres beyond the grid turn left uphill. Cross
   a stile and continue between fencing to a stile to a lane. Cross
   over, pass through a gate into a field and continue ahead: a seat
   halfway across the field allows extensive views of the South
   Downs to be enjoyed in comfort. Turn right at the corner of the
   field, ignore a path on the left and continue down to a junction.
   Turn left along a grassy track to a gate and steps down to a sunken
   path. Cross over and climb steps to a lane. Cross slightly right into
   a field and keep forward, with Tillington Church directly ahead.
   Cross a second field diagonally right to a lane. Pass under a memorial arch into Tillington Cemetery. Follow the main path
   through an avenue of lime and round to a Lychgate. Turn right
   along a road then left onto a raised fenced footpath. Pass the
   Horse Guards Inn and cross over to Tillington Church.

   The beauty of Tillington and its landmark, the unusual 'Scots Crown'
   tower of its parish church, has been captured in paintings by Constable
   and Turner. The inn takes it name from the Horse Guards regiment who
   were billeted in Petworth Park during the Napoleonic Wars.

8. Walk through the church grounds to the far wall. Turn right
   down steps onto a narrow path to the main road. Keep left for 400
   metres to Petworth Park entrance at New Lodge. Keep forward on
   the main gravel path which soon sweeps right along the lower
   end of the lake. At the end of the lake cross the lawn towards the
   left of Petworth House. Leave the park through the gate and tunnel used earlier and retrace the route to Lombard Street and the
   car park.

15. Midhurst and Cowdray Park

Route:	An easy, interesting walk through the fields, woodland and country lanes of Cowdray Estate, including its golf course, polo ground and famous ruins. There is one short ascent along a lane.
Teashop:	The Coffee Pot is part of a complex of small shops in an attractive old building in Knockhundred Row. On the staircase to the coffee shop is a picture depicting the glory of Cowdray House prior to the fire. The coffee shop offers a good selection of homemade cakes and light lunches. Open Monday to Saturday 9.30am – 5.00pm. Sunday 2.30pm – 5.30pm. Closed Sundays from end of October to April. Tel: 01730 815113
Distance:	6 miles.
How to get there:	Midhurst is on the A286 between Haslemere and Chichester.
Public Transport:	Bus services: Stagecoach Hants & Surrey, Stagecoach Coastline.
Start:	GR 885213. Free parking at The Grange car park in the town centre.
Maps:	Landranger 197, Pathfinder 1266 SU82/92, Explorer 133

Midhurst, a traditional market town, nestles between the Downs to the south, the Weald to the north and overlooks the River Rother. Its name, derived from the Saxon Middel Hyrst (middle wood) suggests the town once stood in a clearing of the Wealden forest.

In the Middle Ages a fortified house was built on St Ann's Hill; it was around this house and the market square that the town grew. Although the house is now just a group of stones on a mound, a number of lovely buildings survive in the square; on the north side of the square is the old lock-up and stocks. In Knockhundred Row four 17th century cottages have been sensitively converted to house the public library.

The novelist H.G. Wells lived in the area. He was a pupil and teacher at the Grammar School and also worked for a while in the local chemist's shop. His impressions of life in and around Midhurst are immortalized in many of his novels.

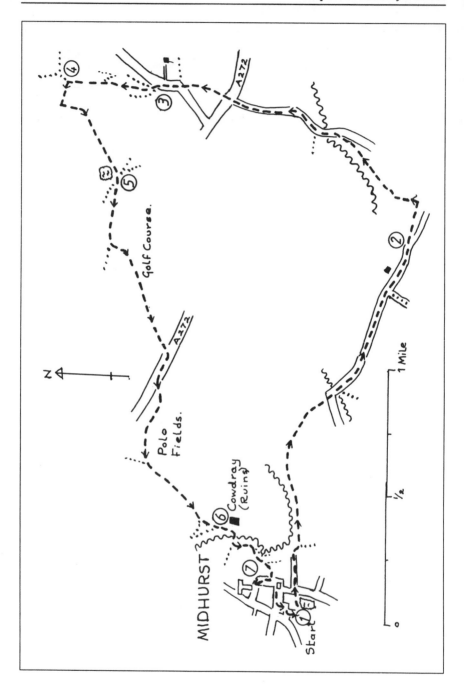

1. Walk down to South Pond at the bottom of the car park and turn left. At the end of the pond cross over to walk down The Wharf. Turn right over a bridge and follow the path round to the left. The path, with the Rother on the left behind trees, eventually leads through gates to a farm. Continue ahead to a road. Cross Costers Brook and continue up this long quiet road to Little Todham Stables.

2. Just beyond the stables, as the road curves, go through a wide gap in the hedge on the left to continue parallel with the road. Ten metres beyond a lone oak turn left across a field then follow the field edge round to the right to cross a stile on the left. Follow the river bank to a gate at a road. Turn left to cross the Rother and continue along a steadily ascending road to the main road (A272). Cross onto a pleasant tree-lined sunken footpath. Turn right at a road.

3. Approximately 15 metres beyond a drive to a house on the right, turn left through a wide sandy gap. Follow the (initially) grassy path between two sandy tracks; the path soon leads through woodland.

4. At a three-way signpost turn left to cross a stile. (If you reach a fork with an island of 3 trees in the centre you have walked 25 metres too far!) With a hedge on the right cross a field then turn left alongside a small copse on the right. At the end of the copse cross a stile on the right. Head slightly diagonally left across a field, pass a pond on the right and leave the field by a gate on the left.

5. Ignore two paths on the left and an ascending track at the side of the field and bear right onto a grassy path between trees. Bear left at a fork to emerge at a golf course. The path crosses a fairway to a shelter at the 15th tee and continues alongside the 8th fairway, following a line of ancient oak trees, to the road (A272). Turn right to the brow of the hill and cross into a field (from here there is a lovely view of Cowdray Ruins). Cross diagonally right to a stile on the right and follow the path round the polo ground. Continue first along a gravel track, then a road, to the front of the ruins.

Cowdray Ruins was once a magnificent Tudor house. Built in about 1530, from local sandstone, it was said to rival the splendour of Hampton Court Palace: both Edward VI and Queen Elizabeth I were entertained here. In 1543 the estate was inherited by Sir Anthony Browne, who during the dissolution had been cursed for his insulting behaviour towards the nuns of Easebourne Priory. The curse said that the house and descendants of Sir Anthony would perish by fire and water. The family lived in peace until 1793: preparations were being made for the wedding of the young Viscount when smouldering rubbish left undetected by workmen caused a fire; a combination of strong winds and the late arrival of the fire crew led to the house being burned to the ground. A week later the Viscount was drowned in a holiday accident. The estate was inherited by his sister Elizabeth who had two sons: they were both drowned in holiday accidents in 1815.

Cowdray ruins

6. Turn right over a bridge then left to follow the river bank. At a fork bear right and climb a footpath via steps. The path bears right to St Ann's Hill and continues to the road. Cross Market Square, turn right into Church Hill and continue to Knockhundred Row and the Coffee Pot.

7. Return along Church Hill, turn right into West Street then left at Grange Road to the car park.

16. Iping Common and Trotton

Route: This pleasant level walk over sandy tracks includes a visit to the beautiful Trotton church. A lovely walk for any season with either the spring gorse, late summer heather or autumn colour: a clear winter's day should provide splendid views.

Teashop: Fitzhall Manor, built in the 1550s, was once the Manor House of Iping. From the elegant tea room, in which only the best china is used, there is a beautiful view across the garden to the Downs. The nine acre garden containing herbaceous borders and a walled herb garden, plus a small farm for children to enjoy is open to the public for a fee. The tearoom can be visited without payment. Open every day 10.00am – 6.00pm (closed Christmas & New Year). Tel: 01730 813634

Distance: 4½ miles.

How to get there: From the A272 between Midhurst and Petersfield take the Elsted turning. The car park is 300 metres on the right.

Public Transport: Bus services: Stagecoach Hants & Surrey, Stagecoach Coastline.

Start: GR 852220. Iping Common Car Park.

Maps: Landranger 197, Pathfinder 1266 SU82/92, Explorer 133

1. With your back to the car park entrance take the first footpath on the right. Turn left for a pleasant stroll along a broad track across the common. At the second crossing turn right (before turning there is a seat on the left for admiring the lovely view). An OS trig point is passed in approximately 15 metres. At a signpost continue to the right and in approximately 120 metres bear left between the gorse to the road.

2. Cross diagonally left into a lay-by and straight ahead into a field. Continue ahead over the brow of a hill and turn left to follow the hedgerow to the corner. The path continues ahead, with fields on the left and trees on the right, soon over a stile and later a footbridge to a road.

3. Turn left. At the end of Whites Farm turn right along a footpath

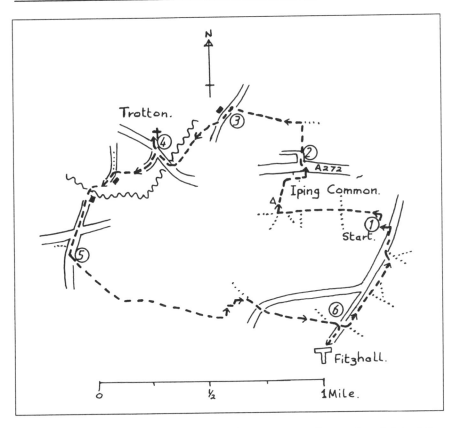

and over a stile. Cross a field and go over a stile on the right of the brow. Turn left: follow the path gradually downfield and between oak trees to cross a stile to a road (if the path is not clear the stile is approximately 40 metres down from a house on the left. A walk down to the river before crossing the stile gives a good view of Trotton Bridge). Turn right along this busy road for a few metres to cross Trotton Bridge and visit St George's church.

Trotton Bridge spans the western end of the Rother. A fine sandstone structure of five semi-circular arches with four large cutwater buttresses on each side, it was built about 1400 by Lord Camoy, who was also responsible for the building of St George's church. The early 14th century church is covered with exquisite wall-paintings dating from that period. They include Christ in Judgment seated on a rainbow, Moses bear-

Mill-workers' cottages

ing Tablets of Law, The Seven Deadly Sins and a remarkable Seven Acts of Mercy depicting such acts as tending the sick and feeding the hungry. The church has two magnificent brasses. In the centre of the chancel is a handsome table tomb brass commemorating Lord Camoy and his second wife: on the floor of the nave is an elegant brass of Margaret de Camoy, dated 1310 it is the earliest full-length brass in England to portray a woman.

4. From the church cross to a footpath by a telephone box. The path curves right and soon changes to a wide grassy track between fencing. At a T-junction turn left, passing some lovely 14th century cottages originally built for the mill-workers. Go through a gate and follow the footpath through Terwick Mill. At the road turn left to a T-junction. Turn right then left towards Elsted. After approximately 150 metres turn left into a field.

5. Cross diagonally right to the right of a plantation. Turn left alongside the plantation. The path continues in the same direction to a farm track. Cross the track, go through a gate and follow the per-

imeter of the fields to cross a footbridge on the right. Turn left: when almost at the bottom of the field bear right behind two oak trees to a stile on the right. Turn right to a road. Cross diagonally left to a footpath through Fitzhall Plantation. On reaching a metal driveway turn right to Fitzhall Manor.

6. From Fitzhall return to the crossing path and turn right. After 25 metres turn left. Continue ahead at a crossing. At a T-junction turn left to the road. Turn right for 250 metres to the car park on the left.

---

17. Cocking, South Downs and Heyshott Down

Route: A quite strenuous but lovely walk. The views are particularly beautiful and the paths are well defined. There are two steady climbs plus a short steep descent which can be quite slippery when wet.

Teashop: Moonlight Cottage Tea Room and Gallery is a welcoming, cosy tea room with an attractive tea garden. The Gallery, a browser's delight, sells antiques, jewellry and paintings. The menu offers morning coffee, homecooked lunches, cream teas and during the summer months, a Saturday barbecue. Open Wednesday to Sunday and Bank Holiday Mondays 10.30am to 5.00pm. Tel: 01730 813336

Distance: 5 miles.

How to get there: Cocking is south of Midhurst on the A286. The car park is half a mile beyond the village.

Public Transport: Bus services: Stagecoach Hants & Surrey, Stagecoach Coastline.

Start: GR 875167. Free public car park on the A286 at the crossing of the South Downs Way.

Maps: Landranger 197, Pathfinder 1286 SU81/91, Explorer 120

---

1. From the pedestrian exit cross the road to follow the South Downs Way for 1½ miles. The track gradually ascends to pass a farm (note the tap in the wall and the notice giving the next drinking point for long-distance walkers). Beyond the farm the ascent steepens (look back for the lovely views towards Buriton). The track eventually levels out and passes two sets of crossing paths.

2. At a third crossing path (leaving the Way) turn left over a stile to cross to an OS trig point (here there are splendid views north over the Weald towards the mast on Bexley Hill and to Blackdown). Continue ahead to cross a stile onto Heyshott Down (the lovely views here are to Heyshott and Midhurst). The path descends quite steeply for a few metres then bears right gradually descending through the Nature Reserve.

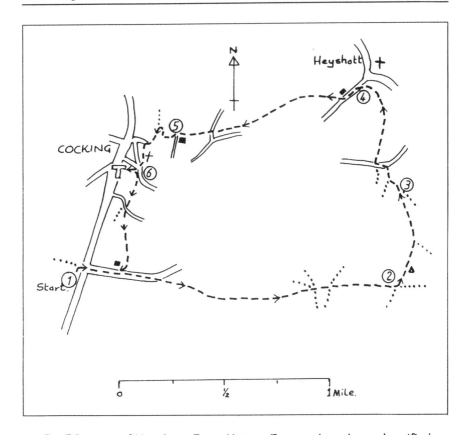

The 50 acres of Heyshott Down Nature Reserve have been classified as
an Area of Outstanding Natural Beauty and a Site of Special Scientific
Interest. In the past the grassland was controlled by grazing sheep; today, management teams re-coppice hazel and cut back ash and scrub to
maintain open downland turf. The rich variety of plants in the chalk grassland include the bee orchid, scabious and rare mosses. Most of the woodland comprises young ash with small pockets of beech, yew and coppiced
hazel. Among the many butterflies who breed on the Down are the
Chalkhill Blue and the Marbled White.

3. Turn left at a T-junction to continue descending. At a fork turn
left and after 100 metres turn right over a stile to go straight across
a field. Cross a footbridge, go diagonally left across a field, heading towards a church, then turn left to the road.

The South Downs Way at Cocking Hill

Heyshott's most famous resident was the reformer Richard Cobden. Born there in 1804, he later moved to Lancashire and set up a calico printing business. An ardent supporter of free trade; he fought for the repeal of the Corn Law of 1815 and was a leading figure in the Anti-Corn Law League inaugurated in Manchester in 1838. His fight continued from Parliament when in 1841 he was elected Member for Stockport. When the Law was finally repealed in 1846 his name was celebrated throughout Europe. However, the long battle had left him financially ruined and it was only through the goodwill of others that he was able to buy a small house in his beloved Heyshott from where he continued his efforts to improve the standard of living of the working community. In St James' church there is a memorial to him on the south wall, a plaque in the front pew marks his seat.

4. Turn left along the road to continue beyond farm buildings. Turn right over a stile by a house 'The Old Thatch'. Continue ahead across two fields. Bear slightly left across a small field to walk through a small copse. Go diagonally left across a large field to a

signpost approximately 70 metres to the right of a lone oak then follow the field edge to a stile. Turn right into a lane and after 5 metres turn left over a stile. Cross a field to Sages Barn.

5. Cross slightly left to follow the perimeter of a field round and take a narrow path on the left with steps down. Turn left onto a narrow path. At a drive turn left, cross a bridge and at a barn turn left to follow the footpath through the church to the south gate. Cross to the footpath opposite which leads to the tea rooms.

6. Return to the church, turn right in front of the memorial then immediately right onto a track. The track steadily ascends to a farm. Turn right to follow the track back to the car park.

---

18. Bosham

Route: A delightful and completely level walk along Bosham Creek, through
                    the nature reserve at Mill Pond and over large open fields. The small
                    amount of road walking should not detract from its enjoyment.If starting
                    the walk from Fishbourne Station, walk down to the A259 and pick up
                    the instructions in paragraph number three.

Teashop: There are two tea shops in Bosham – both extremely popular at
                    week-ends.
                    The Coffee Shop in the Craft Centre is open every day 10.00am –
                    5.30pm in summer and 5.00pm in winter. Tel: 01243 572475
                    Mariners Coffee Shop, overlooking the Quay, is also open every day
                    10.30am – 6.00pm in summer and until 5.00pm in winter. Tel: 01243
                    572960

                    Both sell excellent homemade cakes and light lunches.

Distance: 5 miles.

How to get there: From Chichester take the A259 to the B2146. Turn left for one mile to
                    Bosham Quay.

Public Transport: Bus services: Stagecoach Coastline. Trains: Connex South Central.

Start: GR 806040. Bosham Quay car park.

Maps: Landranger 197, Pathfinder 1305 SU80/90, Explorer 120

The history of Bosham is tied to its position on the fringe of
Chichester Harbour. Local tradition states it is from these shores
King Canute demonstrated his inability to control the tides, and that
his daughter is buried in the vicinity of Holy Trinity Church. In 1865
a small stone coffin was excavated at the alleged burial spot: found
to contain the remains of a child aged about 8 years, it was generally
accepted as proof that she was indeed the King's daughter. It was
from Bosham Creek that King Harold sailed for France in 1064 for
his talks with William of Normandy: a meeting which culminated in
his enforced oath of allegiance and led inevitably to the invasion of
England in 1066. In the church is a copy of that section of the
Bayeaux Tapestry which shows Harold entering the church to pray

Bosham quay

for guidance before setting sail. The beautiful Saxon church exudes an aura of peace and protection: the ancient crypt was used by a small group of Irish monks as early as AD681; crosses on the inner porch indicate where Crusaders blunted their swords after battle as a dedication to peace and it is probable the tower was used as a place of safety for women and children during the Danish raids.

Today Bosham is a haven for yachtsmen, artists and tourists: flood barriers at the gates of cottages bear testament to the continuous battles against the incoming tides!

1. Return to the road. Turn left then left again down a passage parallel with the waterfront. Follow the harbour wall to Harbour Road by the green. Turn left to a junction then cross diagonally left onto a pathway (the path is marked No Right Of Way but this does not apply to pedestrians). Turn left along a road with open fields on the right. At the T-junction turn right along the road.

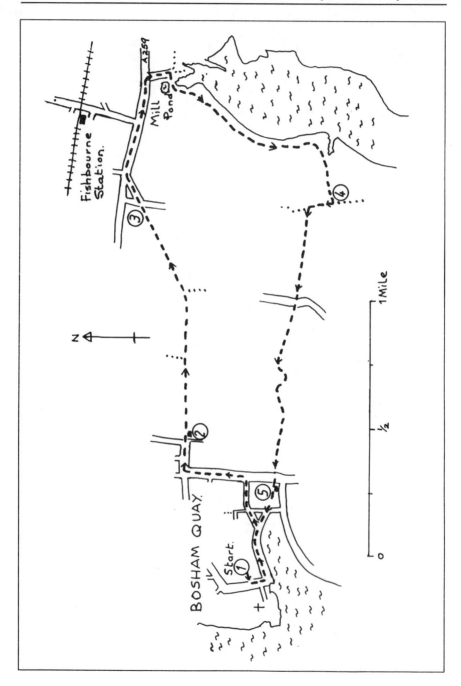

2. On reaching a drive to Refectory Farm take a wide grassy track on the left of a cottage. This long straight track leads past greenhouses and through farmland; it eventually crosses a track and follows a long line of poplars to a road.

3. Continue along the road to the A259. Turn right for approximately half a mile to Mill Lane. Turn right to Mill Pond. Follow the path round the pond and through a small nature reserve. Turn left at the end of the reserve and follow the harbour path on the left. The path leaves the harbour and bears right between oak trees, it passes a tidal pond on the right and continues through scrub to a field. Continue ahead following the field boundary to a three-way signpost.

4. Turn right to a further three-way signpost. Turn left along a field edged with poplars. When the line of poplars turns right continue ahead on a wide grassy path. Cross a road and continue along field boundaries to a gravel track. Continue ahead. Where the track curves left turn right then immediately left (over 2 footbridges) to cross a field to a road.

5. The path continues down the drive of a house 'Byways' to end at the harbour front. Turn right to return to Bosham Quay and the Craft Centre.

   Bosham Walk Craft Centre comprises a collection of shops and showcases displaying arts, crafts, fashion and antiques in an old world setting. There is a resident artist's studio and a fascinating clock restorer – it is a wonderful place for browsing.

19. Walberton and Slindon

Route:	This is an easy level walk through woods, fields and the picturesque village of Slindon. From here, at less then 200 metres above sea level, there is a magnificent view to the sea. It is most interesting if walked in autumn when Top Road Nursery has a brilliant display of pumpkins.
Teashop:	Unfortunately Beam Ends teashop, which was the focus of this walk when this book was first published has closed down. However, three public houses are passed en-route. All serve meals, bar snacks and tea and coffee. Currently they are not 'all-day pubs' – so plan your walk accordingly!
Distance:	5½ miles.
How to get there:	Walberton is between Chichester and Arundel. Turn off the A27 onto the B2132.
Public Transport:	Bus services: Stagecoach Coastline.
Start:	GR 973059. Walberton village hall car park.
Maps:	Landranger 197, Pathfinder 1305 SU80/90, Explorer 121

1. From the car park cross the road and follow the road signs to St Mary's church.

   The churchyard contains two unusual headstones. The first, on the right as you approach the church, depicts how Charles Cook lost his life in 1767 when a tree fell on him; it shows Charles beneath the tree watched over by a horror-struck woodman, Old Father Time, an angel and a skeleton. The second headstone on the south of the church, portrays the death in 1802 of eight year old Ann Rusbridger when a barrel fell from a cart and landed on her.

2. Leave the churchyard via a kissing gate. Cross a field diagonally right towards the end of a row of houses and exit by a gate to a road. Turn right then left into Pound Road and left at Homefield Crescent to cross to a path between bungalows. At a road turn right then cross a road to go down West Walberton Lane.

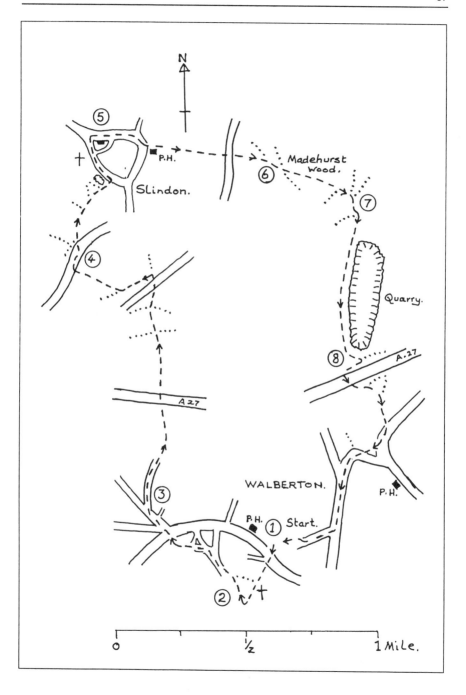

3. Turn right at Copse Lane: the lane soon changes to a path bordering fields. At the main road (A27) cross to a bridleway opposite and continue ahead between fences. Cross a track between gates to enter Slindon Common. Continue ahead at the next two crossing paths. On reaching a road (A29) cross diagonally right to an NT sign and turn immediately left onto a footpath. Ignore a path on the left and continue along the main track until reaching a road.

4. Turn right to enter a car park and take a footpath at the right-hand corner (barrier gated). At a junction take a right fork to emerge at Slindon Pond and a road. Turn left (passing a thatched train carriage in a garden on the right) to Slindon village.

Bequeathed to the National Trust in 1948 together with 3,000 acres of Slindon Estate, this picturesque village has a collection of lovely 17th century flint cottages, a pretty duck pond, majestic beech woods and a view to the sea from the open fields. The parish church of St Mary con-

Thatched railway carriage (Note: this is in a private garden and can only be viewed from the road.)

tains the only wooden effigy in the county; a 5 foot (1.5m) oak figure in plate armour, it represents Sir Anthony St Leger who died in 1539.

Mr and Mrs Upton of Top Road Nursery initially grew beans and radishes for top London restaurants. An experiment 30 years ago of growing marrows led to their present success. From over 20,000 plants a year 30 varieties each of pumpkin and squash are harvested: visitors travel from near and far to see their magnificent autumnal displays.

5. Turn right at the T-junction to pass Top Road Nursery and a number of fine houses, including Bleak House – once the home of the writer and poet Hillaire Belloc. Turn down a lane on the left of a public house to first cross a children's play area then fields (from where on a clear day the sea can be seen) and a fenced garden to reach a road (A29). Cross to a stile and steps then keep ahead over two more stiles to enter Madehurst Wood.

6. At a junction turn right, passing a scout camping area. Continue ahead at a forked crossing path just beyond the camp and ignore all paths off until reaching a four-way crossing.

7. Turn right downhill. In approximately 65 metres the track bears left between two beech trees and passes a three-way signpost. The track soon leads between coppiced chestnut then crosses a wide gravel track at the disused Slindon quarry. Follow the wooden fencing round the quarry to a metal road (once the main road – note the faded white lines and marks left by the cats' eyes). Turn right to descend to a road (A27).

8. Cross to a footpath opposite and turn left alongside a fence. After about 100 metres take a right fork and continue right at a junction, soon crossing a field. At a road turn right for 100 metres then right again onto a narrow path through woodland to a road. Turn right along the road to a junction then turn left towards Walberton. Turn right into Avisford Park Road. The road soon becomes a footpath leading to a playing field. Turn right through a gate into the playing field and walk down to the car park.

20. Arundel

Route: A fairly strenuous walk through beautiful landscape. A pleasant
                    riverside stroll is followed by a rewarding climb over the Downs. There
                    are spectacular views at all stages of the walk and on a clear day the
                    sea is visible from Arundel Park.

Teashop: Set among the antique and gift shops in Tarrant Street, The Copper
                    Kettle is the quintessential English tea shop. A 480 year history,
                    open-beamed dining rooms and a winner, for its pretty courtyard, of
                    Arundel's Summer in Bloom competition. Excellent home-cooked
                    lunches and cakes and scones with fresh cream are all available here.
                    It is open daily 10.00am – 5.00pm. Closed Christmas and New Year.
                    Tel: 01903 883679.

Distance: 7¾ miles.

How to get there: Arundel is 10 miles east of Chichester on the A27.

Public Transport: Bus services: Stagecoach Coastline. Trains: Connex South Central.

Start: GR 021069. Public car park opposite the police station on Queen
                    Street or roadside parking in Mill Road.

Maps: Landranger 197, Pathfinders 1306 and 1287, Explorer 121

Arundel, guarded by a fairy-tale castle and a Gothic Cathedral, has a long history: the town is mentioned in the will of Alfred the Great in 899. Its name is derived from an old French word, the modern form of which is 'hirondelle', meaning little swallow, indicating that it had connections with France long before the Norman Conquest.

The main street, lined with a wealth of tourist's shops, climbs to the magnificent Cathedral of Our Lady and St Philip. Commissioned by Duke Henry XV in 1868, it was designed by Joseph Hansom, the inventor of the Hansom cab. Originally a Parish Church, it was created a Cathedral when the Diocese of Arundel and Brighton was formed in 1965. Philip Howard, falsely accused of treason in 1588, was incarcerated in the Tower of London for 11 years until his death there at the age of 39. He was canonized in 1970; a shrine housing his remains is in the North Transept. Over the West Door is a beautiful

Rose Window. The Cathedral is transformed each year on the Festival of Corpus Christi when an estimated 30,000 flowers are used to carpet the 93 foot (28m) aisle. This tradition, introduced in 1877, is unique to the Cathedral.

Arundel Castle was built in the 11th century by Roger de Montgomery, Earl of Arundel. For over 700 years it has been the seat of the Dukes of Norfolk and Earls of Arundel. During the Civil War the castle was besieged by Parliamentary forces who in six weeks wreaked more damage than all the battles of the preceding 500 years. The castle was left in ruins until the late 1800s when Henry, the 15th Duke of Norfolk, restored it to its present glory. The Gatehouse, Keep, Barbican and a small section of the south wall are all that remains of the original building. Among the many fine treasures on show is the tiny necklace which Anne Boleyn removed from her slender neck, to give to her maid, on the day she was beheaded.

1. Cross a stile at the end of the car park and turn right to follow the riverbank: or from the town end of Mill Road cross the bridge over the river Arun and take the footpath left between Bridge Cottage and Bridge House to follow the riverbank. As the river bends look back for a splendid view of the church and castle. The riverside is followed for some time until reaching a lone white house on the right at a level crossing.

2. Cross the railway track and turn left by the house. Follow the footpath between trees, through a gate and shortly to a field. Cross diagonally to a three-way signpost. Turn left over a stile and continue ahead to two stiles. Cross the stile on the right to follow a tributary of the river. Shortly leave it via the 63 steps (once 70) known as Jacob's Ladder. Continue along the footpath and through a cricket ground to Burpham.

The footpath marks the boundary of an ancient burh, or earthworks, from which the name Burpham is derived. It is said that Jacob's Ladder was used by smugglers as a route from the river to the inn. Burpham has a lovely 12th century church, an 18th century inn, one almost hidden thatched cottage, and a cricket ground from where is possibly the loveliest view from a pitch in the county. These all come together at the crossroads, making it the epitome of the idealized English village.

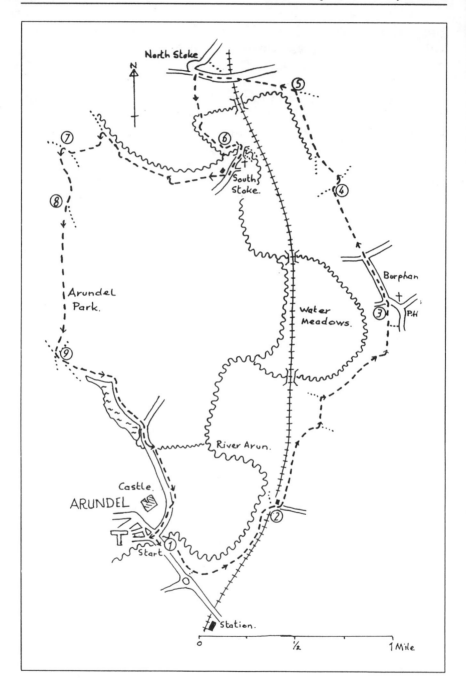

3. Turn left then first right along a road (currently bison are grazing in one of the fields on the left). At Peppering Farm continue ahead through the farmyard then along a grassy track.

4. After passing through a wide metal gate, take the second footpath left. Cross a footbridge and turn right. The footpath meanders through woodland with water meadows on either side.

5. Cross a stile and turn left onto a track. Go through a gate and gradually ascend to a road. Turn left: just before reaching a telephone box turn left onto a narrow footpath. Cross a track and continue ahead shortly crossing a suspension footbridge and continuing through woodland in the water meadows.

6. Cross a stile, turn left and cross the bridge over the Arun. Continue along a gravel track which soon becomes a road. Turn right at a junction then right again at the end of South Stoke Farm. At a barn turn left: the track follows a right-hand field boundary then descends between trees to a stile into a field. Turn right, follow the path uphill and over a stile. Descend through woodland and shortly follow the river on the right and a flint wall on the left to a kissing gate in the wall. Pass through this into the park. Turn sharp left to follow the wall back for about 75 metres then bear right for a steady climb.

Arundel Park was created by the 11th Earl of Arundel in 1787. It offers over 1,000 acres of the best downland in Sussex for the public to explore: the spring fed lake which once turned a Saxon mill is now home to a variety of waterfowl. The beauty of the park has been portrayed by many artists, including Constable and Turner.

7. At a junction turn right onto a stony track then left at a signpost for a fairly strenuous climb. Go through a gate and follow the direction of a signpost over the rise of a hill. Continue along the crest of the hillside to go through a gate.

Hiorne Tower in the distance on the left was designed by an architect Francis Hiorne: it was built in 1787 as a sample in the hope that it would win Hiorne the contract to re-build the castle. Sadly he died two years later at the age of 45. The tower once lived in is now derelict.

View to the South Downs from Arundel Park

8. Five metres from the gate turn right and bear slightly diagonally left downhill. The path is not clear and you should head towards the distant tower; soon you will pass a signpost two metres left of two trees. Continue in the same direction bearing downhill to a stile then follow the track to a junction.

9. Turn left and follow a track to Swanbourne Lake; the track follows the lakeside to the restaurant. Leave the park via a gate and turn right along Mill Road. Just before the bridge take the steps on the left onto a footpath parallel with the road. From Town Bridge turn right to the town centre or left to the car park.

21. Highdown Hill, Highdown Gardens & Patching

Route: Even though there is a constant roar of speeding traffic as the route passes under the A27, this is a lovely walk. Gently undulating downland and field paths give rise to extensive views of the South Downs and, on a clear day, to the Isle of Wight, the Seven Sisters and Arundel. If you haven't visited it before, do allow time to enjoy the beautiful Highdown Chalk Garden.

Teashop: Highdown Tea Room is cosy and quaint with a 'sale table' by the door and a service counter which is constantly replenished with a never-ending supply of homemade cakes and scones from the kitchen. Light meals such as baked potatoes or 'anything' with chips are also served. There are seats outside. Open daily, except Christmas Day and Mondays in winter. April-September 10.00am-5.00pm. October-March until 4.30pm. Tel: 01903 246984.

Distance: 4¾ miles.

How to get there: Highdown Hill is on the A259 approximately 4 miles west of Worthing.

Public transport: Bus service: Stagecoach Coastline.

Start: GR 098041. Highdown Hill car park (free).

Maps: Landranger 197 & 198, Pathfinder 1306 TQ00/10, Explorer 121.

Highdown Hill is the site of an Iron Age Fort; its ramparts enclose one of the earliest known Anglo-Saxon burial ground in England. Both have been excavated and the finds are in Worthing Museum. The Miller's Tomb is that of an eighteenth-century eccentric miller, John Oliver, who built the tomb himself 27 years before he died. Oliver was also a smuggler and legend says that he used the tomb for storing contraband.

1. Enter Highdown Hill from the left-hand corner of the car park. Bear left round the perimeter of Highdown Gardens and ascend towards the Miller's Tomb.

The Miller's Tomb

2. Keeping right of the tomb head towards two Worthing Council signs and pass through a gap in the low flint wall on the left. Ascend alongside a wire fence for 40 metres, keep ahead for 10 metres then bear right. Reach a crossing path with a Highdown Hill sign and turn right onto a wide bridleway to descend first through woodland then between fields. On reaching a crossing track continue ahead for 55 metres then turn left along a gravel track leading to the A280. Cross over and turn left along an equestrian track parallel with the road. At a T-junction turn right to the A27 underpass.

3. From the underpass continue along the lane to a road. Cross over to the Horse & Groom Public House and take a footpath on the right of its play area. Reach a gate to Patching Pond (a private fishing lake) and turn left to a stile into a field. Follow the left-hand hedgerow until reaching a stile in the hedgerow. Here bear right across the field to a stile into a field. Now head across to a squeeze stile but do not go through it. Instead, turn sharp left, recross the

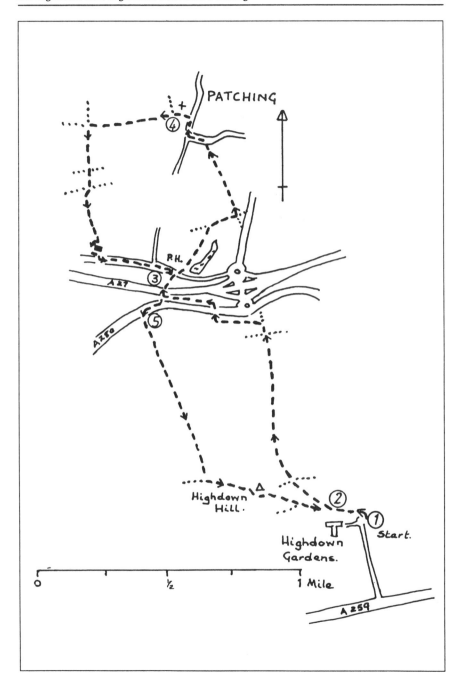

field and return to the field left previously. Bear right to a stile in the top corner. Cross into a field and bear diagonally left. Pass through an opening on the left of some houses, join a road and turn left to a T-junction. Turn right, immediately passing two thatched cottages on the right then reaching a wide concrete farm drive on the left: the drive also leads to the Church of St John the Divine.

4. Turn left along the drive, pass between two barns and cross the farmyard to enter a field. Continue alongside a wire fence on the left and head towards a wood. Cross a stile into the wood and turn left along its perimeter. Enter a field and cross towards a signpost and some distant farm buildings: the path veers very slightly left towards the signpost. Turn left at the signpost and descend towards woodland. Ascend through the wood, keeping ahead at a crossing track. Immediately on leaving the wood, cross a stile on the right into a field. Turn left alongside the boundary, pass a small plantation on the left and head towards some houses. At the top of the field pass through a metal gate into a small field and go straight across to a white house. Respecting the privacy of the owner, follow the right of way through the garden and alongside the house. Leave via a wrought iron gate and go down the driveway to the road. Cross over and turn left along the road. Turn right opposite the Horse & Groom, pass under the A27 again and keep ahead to the A280. Cross over and turn right for 120 metres to a stile on the left into a field.

5. Continue alongside a chainlink fence on the right to a planked footbridge. Over the bridge turn left and ascend alongside the right-hand boundaries of two large fields via a stile. At the top of the second field, cross a stile into an area of scrub. After 17 metres fork right for 30 metres to a crossing path with a Highdown Hill sign. Turn left along the hill and head for the trig point at the summit. Here turn right along the ridge of the Hill Fort. Leave the fort via seven well-worn steps and keep ahead, gradually descending to the gap in the wall used earlier. From here, retrace the route back to the car park, the gardens and the tea room.

In spring, Highdown Garden is approached along a quarter of a mile drive banked by thousands of magnificent daffodils – a promise of the delights in store. This exquisite, intimate garden was the creation, over 50 years, of Lord & Lady Stern: they worked together with infectious dedication to prove that diverse plants would grow happily in chalk. The garden, set in a chalk pit in parts 9 metres (30 feet) high, offers a unique collection of rare plants and trees and has been deemed a National collection. However, this is not just a garden for professionals – to wander round a succession of snowdrops, crocus, daffodils and anemones and later, hellebores followed by paeonies and later still roses, is a joy not to be missed. The garden, gifted by Lord & Lady Stern to Worthing Borough Council, is open daily from April-September 10.00am-6.00pm. From October-March it is open Monday-Friday only, 10.00am-4.00pm. Admission is free.

```
┌─────────────────────────────────────────────────────────┐
│                                                           │
│           22. Chanctonbury Ring                           │
│                                                           │
└─────────────────────────────────────────────────────────┘
```

Route: Quiet country lanes, one easy woodland climb, and gentle undulating downland culminate in the magnificent views from Chanctonbury Ring, the main feature of this lovely walk.

Teashop: Wiston Post Office and Tea Shop is truly rural. It has a cottage garden with a stream and wooden bridges. In an adjoining paddock ducks, geese, goats, pigs and ponies graze. The tea shop serves homemade soup and light lunches and a delectable assortment of homemade cakes and scones. Open Monday to Friday (closed Wednesday) 10.30am – 5.00pm. Saturday & Sunday 10.30am – 5.30pm.Tel: 01903 892330

Distance: 6 miles.

How to get there: From Storrington follow the A283 towards Steyning. Immediately beyond the A283/A24 roundabout turn left into Sandhill Lane.

Public Transport: Bus services: Stagecoach Coastline.

Start: GR 121134. Roadside parking in Sandhills Lane (cul-de-sac).

Maps: Landranger 198, Pathfinder 1287 TQ01/11, Explorer 121

1. Cross the A283, turn right to the roundabout and take a footpath by the Worthing road sign. The path runs parallel to the A24 then veers left between trees to a lane.

2. Turn left to walk through Washington village. At the junction turn right to Stocks Mead. Cross the road to go over a stile on the left into a field. Cross a stile on the right within five metres then cross a field diagonally left to enter a wood via 12 steps. The path ascends through the wood then follows fields on the left to the junction with the South Downs Way.

3. Turn left onto the wide track and in about 10 metres continue left at a fork. On reaching a three-way signpost, the track begins to climb: continue to the next signpost which is a few metres in front of a gate, bear left through the gate to climb Chanctonbury Hill.

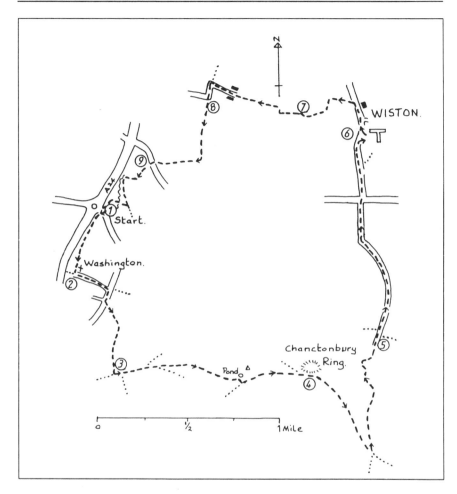

The path soon goes between disused pits then climbs to a gate. Go through the gate and continue ahead over the rise and across open downland to a gate in wire fencing. Through the gate is a pretty dew pond and the first view of Chanctonbury Ring. Follow the path on the right of the pond to a track. Turn left over a cattle grid and follow the track to Chanctonbury Ring. (If the gate to the pond is impassable, turn right and follow the fence to a gate on the left. The pond is a few metres to the left of the information board.)

Dew ponds, a traditional downland feature, were built from medieval times to the 1930s. 'Dew pond' is a romanticised name for what shepherds called mist, sheep, cloud or fog ponds. The ponds were hammered out by shepherds to collect rain: rolling sea mist and low cloud helped to reduce evaporation, thus ensuring a longer-lasting supply of water for the many sheep which roamed the Downs. This Dew pond, first constructed about 1870, was restored by the Society of Sussex Downsmen in 1970 to commemorate European Conservation Year.

Chanctonbury Ring (783ft/189m) once the site of an Iron Age hill fort and a Roman temple, is the most famous landmark on the South Downs. The word 'Ring' properly applies to the earthworks of the fort, not the trees planted by the young Charles Goring of Weston House. In 1760 a ring of beech saplings were planted by Charles when he was just a school boy: his wish was to see them grow to maturity. By the time he died, aged 85, his dream was fulfilled. Sadly the ring was devastated during the October storms of 1987 when over 50% of the trees were either uprooted or irreparably damaged. It is hoped that saplings recently planted by the Countryside Commission will eventually restore the ring to its former glory. On a clear day there are extensive views southwards to Cissbury Ring and the coast and northwards over the Weald.

4. From Chanctonbury Ring the track curves right, crosses a cattle grid and descends to a crossing path. Turn left to enter a wood. The track descends for a while and eventually makes a hairpin bend to the right (at this point there is a rough track rising to the left). Follow the main track right to soon emerge at a lane.

5. Follow this country lane for about half a mile to the main road. Cross over and continue down Wiston Road to the tea shop.

6. From the tea shop turn right for about a quarter of a mile to a footpath on the left opposite Abbotts House. Cross a stile and keeping to the hedgerow on the right follow the perimeter of a large field.

7. Turn right as the track curves right then go immediately right through a wide gap and follow the direction of a signpost across a field, keeping to the hedgerow on the left. Continue round a copse on the left then go straight across a field towards farm buildings.

Wiston post office and tea shop

Continue between the buildings then along a lane. At a signpost follow the lane left.

8. Leave the lane as it turns right and continue ahead along a grassy path bordering a field. Go through a gate into a wood. Follow the path through until meeting a high wire fence. Turn right alongside the fence then follow the footpath signs through a sand quarry to a road.

9. Cross diagonally right to a footpath on the left of Rock House Nurseries. The path follows the nursery then runs parallel with a stream: watch for a footbridge on the right. Cross the bridge and follow the path through to the parking area.

```
┌─────────────────────────────────────────────────────────┐
│                                                           │
│   23. Ditchling, the South Downs and                      │
│       Clayton                                             │
│                                                           │
└─────────────────────────────────────────────────────────┘
```

Route: This is a superb walk, not long, but so full of interest it is worth allowing plenty of time for. There is one quite steep climb; the ridge walk has beautiful views and the church at Clayton is a delight to visit. The meadow by the windmills is a good picnic spot: lunch can be bought at the Jack and Jill public house.

Teashop: Dolly's Pantry and Old Ditchling Bakery is a 17th century oak-beamed tea room with an attractive walled garden. The cream teas and toasted tea-cakes are excellent. Open all year until 5.00pm. Tel: 01273 842708

Distance: 6¾ miles.

How to get there: From Brighton take the A23 to the junction with the A273. Continue along the A273. Turn right onto the B2112 to Ditchling.

Public Transport: Bus services: Arriva, Autopoint Coaches.

Start: GR 326152. Free parking at Ditchling village hall, Lewes Road.

Maps: Landranger 198, Explorer 122(17), Pathfinder 1288 TQ21/31

---

1. From the car park turn left and left again at South Street. At a road junction cross to a footpath waymarked The Downs. Follow the path between houses into a field and turn left. The path leads through fields along hedgerows and through a farm to a track. Cross the track to walk through a wood and over a stile. Cross a field diagonally left to a stile and turn left along a lane.

2. Cross a parking area and turn right over a stile onto a steeply ascending path. On reaching a stile cross and bear slightly left (a seat just to the left is admirably placed for a rest and view point) to continue uphill. Shortly, the path dips and rises and continues through a gate. On reaching a marker post turn left for a gradual ascent along a grassy path. Cross the South Downs Way to Ditchling Beacon trig point.

   The Beacon (813ft/248m) given to the National Trust in memory of an airman killed in the second world war, is the third highest point on the

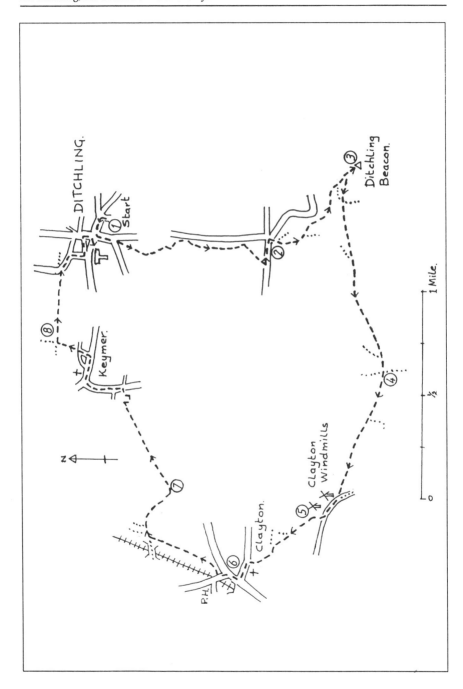

South Downs Way. The site of an Iron Age fort, it was also one of a chain of summits on which beacon fires were lit in 1588 to warn of the approaching Armada. The views west are to Wolstonbury Hill and beyond to Devil's Dyke, on a clear day it is possible to see Chanctonbury Ring.

3. Return to the track and turn left onto the South Downs Way for a beautiful and exhilarating ridge walk.

There are superb views north across the Weald. To the south, on a clear day, it is possible to see the sea. Dew ponds passed en-route are explained in walk no.22. The crossing from East to West Sussex is made when an elegant signpost is reached; pointing the way to Brighton, Keymer, Eastbourne and Winchester, the post is a moving memorial to a young couple who died in 1994.

4. From the signpost, continue ahead. As the track gradually descends the Jack and Jill windmills come into view and soon a car park is reached. Cross into the car park to see the windmills.

100 years ago windmills were a common sight on the Downs. The Jack and Jill windmills survive as prominent downland features. Jack a black brick tower mill was built in 1876. Jill, a white-timbered post mill, was built in Brighton in 1821. 30 years later she was hauled to the Downs by a team of 80 oxen where she continued to work with Jack until 1906. Restored in the 1970s Jill is now producing stone-ground flour and is open to the public on Sundays in summer; Jack is in private ownership.

5. Leave the car park by a gate into a meadow. Turn left to descend to a road. Turn left to the church.

The Norman church of St John the Baptist is renowned for its beautiful wall paintings. Estimated to date from 1080 and representing the Last Judgment, they were used for teaching the Gospels to the uneducated. Possibly the most complete of its date in existence they were discovered during restoration in 1893. A fine smaller reproduction can be seen on the wall below.

The majestic castellated Clayton Tunnel was built in 1846; 1½ miles long, it is a magnificent feat of engineering. On the top in splendid isolation sits a tunnel-keeper's cottage – one cannot help wondering how the nerves of today's inhabitants are affected by the many trains now passing through.

Clayton railway tunnel

6. Turn right at the main road for a short detour to Clayton Tunnel. Cross back to a footpath on the right of the railway. On reaching a bridge and a crossing path cross a stile on the right and take a wide grassy path through a field. Turn right onto a gravel track. Shortly leave the track and cross to a signpost by a garden hedge.

7. Turn left and cross diagonally to the bottom right-hand corner of the field. Continue in the same direction across two fields. Go over a footbridge, cross to the far left corner of a field and follow a fenced path by houses to a road. Turn left along the road then right to follow the main road to Silverdale Road. Turn left down a narrow footpath. Cross a road and bear left through two fields and cross a footbridge into a third field.

8. Turn immediate right along a hedgerow to cross a stile and footbridge on the right. Continue ahead through a field. This field was once part of a Roman road: the view to the right is the north face of the South Downs escarpment – the ridge which you walked earlier. Leave the field by a stile on the left. Turn right

down a lane, pass the village pond and walk through the church grounds to the High Street. Turn right then right again into West Street for the tea shop.

Nestling at the foot of the Downs, Ditchling is a bustling and charming village whose records go back to 765. The manor has been held by Alfred the Great and Edward the Confessor. The oldest building is the 13th century church: built of local flint and Normandy Stone, it contains rare chalk carvings and a massive Norman treasure chest. Below the church steps is Wings Place; a beautiful unusual half-timbered period house, it is said that Henry VIII gave it to Anne of Cleves for agreeing to their divorce.

24. Friston Forest and The Seven Sisters

Route: Possibly the most strenuous in the book, this walk offers a superb mixture of forest, downs, coast and river. The rises and falls of Friston Forest are followed by a stroll across open downland to the coast. The scenic highlight is the spectacular, occasionally strenuous walk over the undulating chalk downland of The Seven Sisters. On a hot day allow time for a dip in the sea at Birling Gap; the hotel there provides good food or you could picnic on the beach. The walk ends with a gentle amble along the meandering River Cuckmere.

Teashop: Situated behind the visitor centre is Exceat Farmhouse Restaurant. Originally a 17th century farmhouse it has a cosy restaurant and a walled courtyard. A good assortment of homemade cakes is offered. Open April to October 10.00am – 5.30pm. November to March 10.30am – 4.00pm. Tel: 01323 870218

Distance: 7 ½ miles.

How to get there: Seven Sisters Country Park is 5 miles west of Eastbourne on the A259.

Public Transport: Bus services: Stagecoach South Coast, Brighton & Hove.

Start: GR 519005. (Pay and Display) Seven Sisters Country Park car park on the A259.

Maps: Landranger 199, Explorer 123(16), Pathfinder 1324 TV49/59/69.

Exceat was an important fishing community during the Middle Ages until it suffered a number of disasters: fierce storms destroyed the moorings used by the fishermen; in the 1340s the Black Death devastated the community and in 1460, after recovering from the earlier disasters, it suffered further destruction at the hands of French raiders. In 1528 the village was incorporated with Westdean. Exceat has an excellent visitor centre in an 18th century converted barn. Next door is the Living World centre: a unique natural history exhibition with live, rare insects and crustaceans.

1. From the car park turn right, cross to the bike hire shop and take the path on the right. Go through a gate and follow the South Downs Way uphill and over stone steps in a wall (a good resting point for admiring the view over the Cuckmere). Turn right then immediately left into Friston Forest. In approximately 20 metres descend a long flight of over 200 steps to the pretty setting of Westdean village pond and cottages. Turn right at Pond Cottage to walk through the village.

   Westdean is a pretty, unspoiled village in the valley bottom of Friston Forest. The forest comprises two thousand acres of mostly deciduous trees, the vast majority being beech. In recent years the southern fringe has been planted with conifers to protect the valuable beech from coastal winds and salt spray. In the 15th century John Cade and his rebels, fighting for the rights of the peasants and on the run from the King's army, sought refuge in the forest.

2. At a fork bear right, the lane leads uphill and back into the forest. Continue along the wide forest track. At a fork take the right track waymarked Friston. Where the track sweeps to the left continue ahead down a slightly grassed track. Cross a gravelled track and ascend to Friston Hill – in their seasons there is an abundance of wild flowers here. Keep to the right of the open grassland of Friston Hill then descend to a road.

3. Turn left, continue beyond the road bend for a few metres to a footpath on the right, parallel to the road and much pleasanter to walk on. At a waymarked post turn right, cross the road and go through a gate into a field. Bear left across a faint path to a gate. Cross a road to a stile opposite and continue slightly diagonally left to the top corner of a field into a wood. The woodland path ascends to the road. Cross over and go down Crowlink (No Through) Road.

   The 11th century Church of St Mary is a simple but interesting church which has been sympathetically altered over the centuries. The churchyard gate is unusual in that it opens either way on a central pivot. Designed in the 19th century by a Sussex blacksmith called Tapsell, it is a reproduction of the original iron gate which was so designed in order to

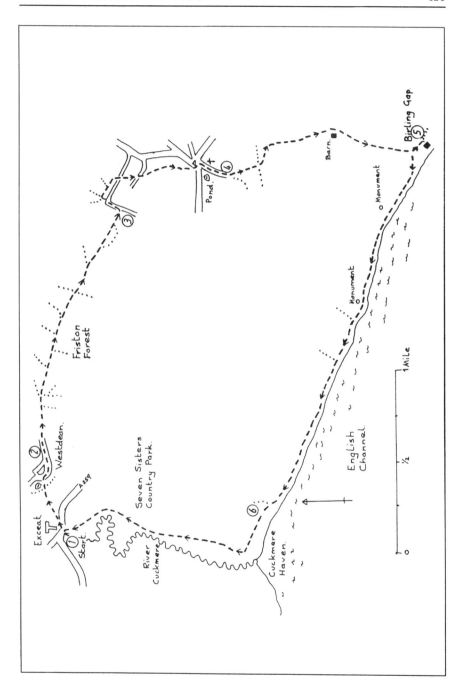

provide a resting place for coffins. Tapsell Gates are peculiar to these parts of Sussex.

Friston Pond, first mentioned in the 17th century, and man-made, has been agreed an Ancient Monument. It became one of the first ponds in England to be so protected.

4. At the Crowlink National Trust (NT) sign turn left through a gate then diagonally cross a field and go through the gate ahead. Turn left along a wire fence. Bear right just before the fence meets a wall to go through a gate on the right of the wall. Follow the scarp on the left to a barn on the horizon. Keeping to the left of the barn, continue straight ahead to the left of a clump of trees. Birling Gap Hotel comes into view on the left in about two minutes. Continue down the field to leave it at a gate. The path continues downhill then along a narrow footpath to the road, where you can see Birling Gap ahead (just before leaving the narrow path you pass a gate on the right, waymarked South Downs Way, where the walk restarts).

Birling Gap is a relatively quiet beach sheltered by high dramatic white chalk cliffs. It is estimated that this stretch of coastline is eroding at the rate of almost a metre a year. Since 1920 three cottages have been demolished to avoid their collapse into the sea. The NT who own Birling Gap have recently erected a viewing platform on the cliff top with steps down for access to the beach.

5. From the hotel retrace your steps to the gate waymarked South Downs Way. Turn left through the gate to begin the beautiful coastal walk over the Seven Sisters.

The Seven Sisters, a heritage coastline and a Site of Special Scientific Interest (SSSI) is acknowledged as the most spectacular chalk coastal scenery in England. There are actually eight sisters but apparently it was decided that 'Seven Sisters' formed a pleasing alliteration! The land, owned by the County Council and the NT is guaranteed to be preserved for public use. The rises and falls of the sisters are quite steep but the downland is beautiful to walk on and any energy expended is amply rewarded by the magnificent views. Wild flowers border the paths in spring, in late summer tiny Chalkhill Blue butterflies constantly dance along.

Cuckmere Haven

Two memorials are passed on the way: the first commemorates the gift of Micheldene Down to the NT by WA Robertson in memory of his two brothers killed in the Great War. The second is a large boulder of Sarsen Stone stranded when the rocks eroded 50 million years ago. A plaque on the stone commemorates a donation to the NT which enabled it to purchase Crowlink Valley: bordered by four of the Seven Sisters it is the largest NT property in East Sussex.

From Haven Brow there is a superb view of Cuckmere Haven, the only unspoilt estuary in Sussex, its air of utter peacefulness is quite breathtaking. The estuary and salt marshes combine to provide an excellent site for bird watching – dunlin, plovers, redshank, heron and many more waders can be seen feeding here.

6. On reaching Haven Brow cross a stile on the left of a signpost and follow the waymarked path round the Saltmarshes, passing a number of pillboxes built to defend the valley during the Second World War. Continue through a gate onto a track and follow the course of the river back to the car park and Exceat Farmhouse Restaurant.

25. Alfriston and
The Long Man of Wilmington

Route: This is a lovely walk with many interesting features. A pleasant stroll through Cuckmere valley is followed by a steady but not difficult climb of about one mile. There are magnificent views along the route.

Teashop: From an abundance of tea shops we chose The Tudor House with its attractive garden and lovely view to the Downs. A licensed restaurant, it offers a variety of homemade cakes, scones and light lunches. If a pot of tea is all you need, the friendly staff are happy to oblige. Open every day 10.30am – 5.30pm summer and until 5.00pm winter. Tel: 01323 870891

Distance: 6 miles.

How to get there: From Lewes take the A27 towards Polegate. After approximately 8 miles turn right to Alfriston.

Public Transport: Bus services: Stagecoach South Coast, Autopoint Coaches.

Start: GR 521033. Public car park.

Maps: Landranger 199, Explorer 123(16), Pathfinder 1324 TV49/59/69.

Alfriston nestles under the Downs in the Cuckmere valley. Its main street is lined with gift shops, tea rooms and old attractive buildings. In Wellington Square is the stump of the ancient market cross, one of only two surviving market crosses in the county. Alfriston thrived during the Napoleonic Wars when the large number of troops in the area had to be catered for: brewers, tanners, harness-makers and many more traders all prospered prior to Wellington's famous victory at Waterloo in 1815. In the early 1800s here, as elsewhere on the coast, smuggling was rife: the many inns providing excellent meeting rooms and hiding places. Smuggler's Inn, a building with six staircases and five exits, was once the home of Stanton Collins; a butcher and ringleader, in 1831 he was sentenced to seven years transportation for his illicit dealings.

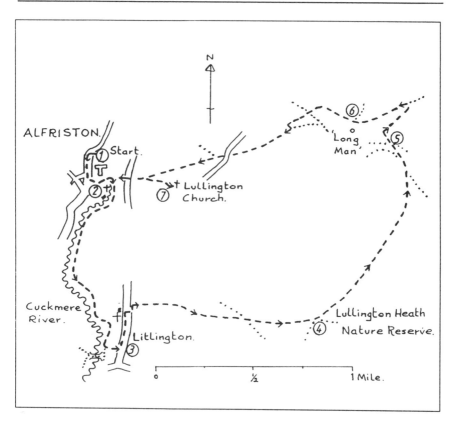

1. From the car park turn left to walk through the village. At the
   United Reform Church turn left onto a footpath leading to the
   church and Clergy House.

   On a Saxon mound on the green, known as the Tye, stands St Andrew's
   Church. Built in the shape of a Greek cross this magnificent 14th century
   church is often referred to as the Cathedral of the Downs. Next to the
   church is the Clergy House, a lovely medieval half-timbered thatched
   priest's house. The first property to be acquired by the National Trust, it
   was bought in 1896 for £10. The main body of the house is a hall open to
   the roof. The floor of the hall was originally made of rammed chalk sealed
   with sour milk. When the Trust renovated the house in 1977 using original
   building techniques, thirty gallons of sour milk were used for the new floor!

2. From the drive to the church bear left to a footbridge over the

The Clergy House, Alfriston

Cuckmere. Turn right onto the South Downs Way and follow the riverbank as it meanders through the meadows. Turn left just before reaching a white painted bridge (first going to the bridge for a lovely view of the White Horse).

The White Horse, a chalk figure in the Downs, was first cut in the 19th century by a farmer who lived at Frog Firle. It was covered during the Second World War to prevent it being used as a landmark.

3. At the road turn left through Litlington. (If you are in need of a break at this point, there is a lovely tea garden here.) At Church Farm turn right onto a track. Turn left after 20 metres then right at a gate. The track ascends steadily for almost a mile to a crossing at a waymarked post and the Lullington Heath Nature Reserve sign.

4. Turn left through the nature reserve. Go through a gate and continue across a field to a further gate. Follow the line of a wire fence over the open downland. Approximately 50 metres before reaching two gates bear right to go through a wooden gate onto Wilmington Hill.

5. Bear left (following the Wilmington sign). The path descends and curves right. Turn sharp left at a fork onto a grassy track to pass the Long Man on the left.

   Cut in the face of the Downs, on Windover Hill, is England's largest chalk figure the Long Man of Wilmington: 240ft (73m) long with a staff in each hand, its origin is surrounded in mystery. Some of the many theories are: he was here 1,000 years before the Saxons; the Saxons made him; he was the work of the Wilmington monks; a fertility figure; and, even, a giant slain in battle! Perhaps it is the not knowing that makes him so interesting. Now outlined in white brick in order to protect the underlying chalk the figure is cared for by Sussex Archaeological Society.

6. The path continues and shortly leads through a gate and across a track. Cross a field and turn left along the field edge. Turn right through a gate onto the South Downs Way: the track descends to a road. Cross to the footpath opposite and within 100 metres cross a stile on the left to go diagonally right across two fields. Cross a stile on the left and turn left uphill to follow the path between trees to Lullington church.

   The church, surrounded by trees in a beautiful peaceful setting, is said to be the smallest church in England. In fact it is the chancel of a much larger, now ruined, 13th century church. It is thought the main church was destroyed in Cromwellian times. The chancel has seats for 20 people but has been known to find room for almost double that number on festival days.

7. Retrace your steps to where you turned left and continue down to a road. Cross to the footpath opposite which leads back to the footbridge by Alfriston church, from where you can wander through the village to either the Tudor House restaurant or one of the many tea rooms in the High Street.

26. Barcombe Mills and the River Ouse

Route: A pleasant level walk through farmland and along the delightful River Ouse as it meanders through the meadows. From the open fields there are lovely views across the countrysid.

Teashop: Unfortunately Barcombe Mills Station Restaurant, which was the focus of this walk when the book was first published has closed down. However, the Anchor Inn with an adjoining Riverside Kiosk is passed en-route. The inn is open all day and serves food at lunchtime. The kiosk serves a variety of sandwiches and ice-creams and hot and cold drinks. It is open 11.00am to 6.00pm daily in the summer, but weekends only in the winter. Tel: 01273 400414.

Distance: 5 miles.

How to get there: Barcombe Mills is approximately 3½ miles from Lewes off the Lewes – Uckfield road (A26). Turn off the A26 at the Barcombe sign. The car park is three-quarters of a mile along on the right.

Public Transport: Bus services: Brighton & Hove.

Start: GR 434146. Free car park by the River Ouse a quarter of a mile west of Barcombe Mills Old Station.

Maps: Landranger 198, Explorer 122(17), Pathfinder 1289.

Today, Barcombe Mills exists in name only. Records show that mills existed here in 1086 and that over the centuries there have been corn, paper and linseed oil mills. The last working mill at Barcombe used water-powered machinery to make buttons; built in 1870 it ceased working in 1934 and was destroyed by fire in 1939. Millstones can still be found along the footpaths nearby.

1. Take the footpath in the left-hand corner of the car park. Turn right over a bridge and just before a second bridge turn right to follow the river Ouse. Cross a footbridge and continue ahead keeping the Ouse on the left.

   The River Ouse has its beginning from many feeders around Ashdown for-

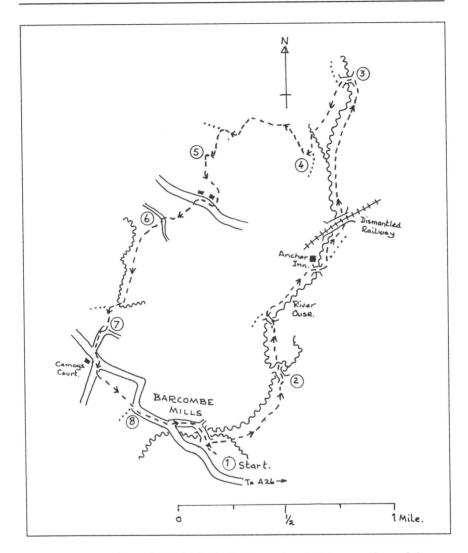

est: it cuts through the high chalk Downs to wind its way through Lewes to the sea at Newhaven. In the past it was a major source of transport across the Weald: Iron-Age boats carried charcoal, anvils, weapons and other wares associated with the Wealden iron industry. A tidal river meandering through the meadows, the Ouse greatly enhances the beauty of the surrounding landscape.

Footbridge over the River Ouse

2. After following the riverbank for a while cross a footbridge, go down a narrow path and over a stile to continue with the river still on the left. Cross a farm bridge on the left of some barns. Turn right onto a tarmac path then left between trees to follow the river again. Cross a wide bridge and turn left over a stile. (This is a picturesque spot where boats are hired and drinks, sandwiches and cakes are sold from a cabin.) The riverside path leads under the disused Lewes to Uckfield railway.

3. Follow the river as it meanders through five fields to a track and a footbridge (just before reaching the track you will see a large bungalow on the right). Cross the footbridge, go through a gate on the left and bear diagonally left across a field to go over a footbridge. Follow a short path up a slight incline and through a gate.

4. Follow the highest path, by a fence on the right, to go over a stile. Continue between hedgerows to a field. Turn right and follow the field boundary to a metal gate and stile. Continue up a large field, turn left at the top and continue along the boundary until reach-

ing an opening on the right. Pass through the opening and follow a copse round two sides, keeping it on your left, to reach a stile into a field.

5. Turn right over the stile and continue along with the field boundary on the right. Turn left at the corner to go over a stile half-way down on the right. Cross a small field to a gate then follow a path up to a stile. Go through a farmyard to a road and turn right. 30 metres beyond a house 'Little Scufflings' turn left over a stile in a hedge to walk up a field and over a stile at the top. Continue downfield then over a stile and footbridge to a road.

6. Cross diagonally left to a stile and cross a field to a stile by a gate. Follow Bevern stream (a tributary of the Ouse) on the right through meadows to cross a footbridge on the right. Continue towards a gate ahead but go through the gate next to it on the left. Cross a field to go over a stile ahead then cross diagonally right up a field and over a stile and footbridge 3 metres to the right of a telephone pole.

7. Turn right onto a gravel track leading through a farmyard to a road. Turn left then first right to a stile opposite a house 'Camoys Court'. The path leads in a continuous line across three fields to a road.

   Barcombe station, on the Uckfield to Lewes line, was built in 1858: the line also served as an alternative route for the Victoria to Brighton service. It was closed in 1969 when its route obstructed the expansion of the motorways.

8. Turn right for approximately 200 metres to a narrow lane in front of houses on the left. Turn right at Barcombe House and cross an old toll bridge (a plaque on the wall states this was the earliest site where tolls were levied in Sussex). Continue along the lane to the car park.

```
┌─────────────────────────────────────────────────────────┐
│                                                           │
│         27. Burwash and Bateman's                         │
│                                                           │
└─────────────────────────────────────────────────────────┘
```

Route: Mixed woodland, meadows, and fine views combine with the
                    opportunity to visit Bateman's, one of the loveliest of all the National
                    Trust houses and once the home of Kipling. There are no steep climbs
                    but the tracks and fields can be very muddy in winter.

Teashop: The Mulberry Tea Rooms at Bateman's is in a pretty walled garden
                    with extra seating on the terrace. Many of the homemade cakes are
                    made from flour ground in the mill at the bottom of the garden. A
                    self-service system operates for light lunches. Open April to October,
                    Saturday to Wednesday 11.00am – 5.30pm. Tel: 01435 882302

                    The Bear Inn, in High Street, serves cream teas daily between 3.00pm
                    and 5.00pm. It has a separate restuarant "The Kipling" and a large
                    garden with magnificent views overlooking the Dudwell Valley. Tel:
                    01435 882540

Distance: 4½ miles.

How to get there: Burwash is on the A265 approximately 5 miles east of Heathfield.

Public Transport: Bus services: RDH Services.

Start: GR 764246. Free public car park adjacent to The Bear Inn.

Maps: Landranger 199, Pathfinder 1270 TQ62/72, Explorers 136 & 124

Burwash is an attractive village with a long wide High Street containing pretty weather-boarded houses. The village supported several thriving forges during the height of the iron industry, evidence of which can be seen in the number of blacksmith signs still in the High Street. The parish church contains the earliest known cast-iron tomb slab, dating from the 14th century. Also in the church is a bronze plaque in memory of Kipling's son John, who died in France during the Great War.

1. From the car park turn left along High Street. Turn right at the Catholic church and go sharp left through a kissing gate onto a drive. Descend to Dawes Oast House then cross a stile at the side of the house. Follow a hedgerow on the right to cross a footbridge.

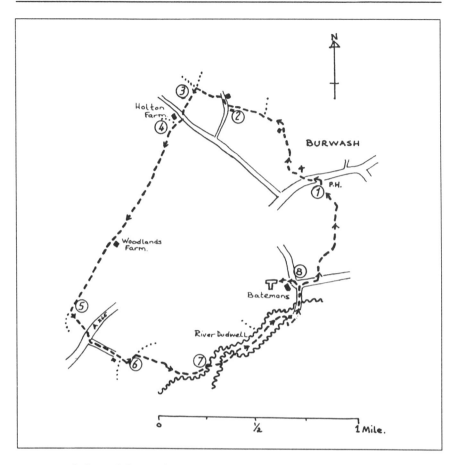

Turn left and head for a white oast house (the area between the
two field gates can be quite muddy). Go through a gate to the lane.

2. Turn right. At the end of the lane, opposite a house, take a narrow
footpath on the left which ascends to an orchard. Turn right and
climb up by the hedgerow to a gap at the top on the right.

3. Go through the gap and turn left along a wide track, soon passing
a memorial to Flight Lieutenant R.F. Rimmer who was killed in
action in 1940. Turn left at a lane to immediately reach Holton
Farm house.

4. At the end of the house turn right onto a grassy bridleway. Ignore
a stile immediately on the right and continue ahead for approxi-

mately two miles. This is a good track with lovely views at intervals on the right but it can be muddy in winter and possibly overgrown in summer. The track eventually climbs through light woodland and passes Woodland Farm on the left. Bear left where the track meets a farm track but first look over the metal gate at the superb views across the Weald towards the Kent border.

5. Just before the track curves left at the top of the hill, turn left at a stone bridleway sign onto an enclosed track. The track leads to the road (A265) and the Burwash Weald village sign. Turn right and cross diagonally right onto a footpath. Continue past Pear Tree Cottage to enter a field. Cross a stile on the left of the field and head diagonally right to a gap in a fence. Follow a metal fence on the left to a gate.

6. Turn right in front of the gate and follow the hedgerow to a stile into a wood. Six metres beyond the stile turn left at a well placed fallen tree trunk – don't fall over the 12" (30cm) high waymarker post! Follow this woodland path to a stile and the River Dudwell. Continue along a field boundary to a footbridge.

7. Cross the footbridge and turn left. (The following fields can be very muddy in winter.) Leave the field by a gate on the right of another gate. Follow the bottom of a field to cross a footbridge on the left. Turn right, still following the stream. Ignore a footbridge on the left and continue ahead to cross a footbridge onto a broad track. This track leads to the beautiful millpond at Bateman's. Walk round the pond to a track. Turn left to walk up to the house.

Dominating the skyline are the magnificent chimney stacks of Bateman's: a lovely mellow house built in the 17th century by a successful ironmaster. When the industry declined it became a farmhouse. It was later restored and in 1902 was sold to Rudyard Kipling who lived there until his death in 1936. The house retains many original features, such as the stone doorways and a beautiful oak staircase. The Kiplings have left many mementos of their Indian travels. From Bateman's Kipling wrote many of his most popular works including If, The Glory of the Garden and Puck of Pook's Hill – the hill of which can be seen from his study. The house, in particular Kipling's study, remains much as it was when they lived there. The gardens and the lovely meadow walk to the millpond were de-

Rudyard Kipling's garden

signed not only to complement the house but also to harmonise with the countryside.

8. Take the lane opposite the front of the house for 200 metres and cross a stile on the left into a field. Follow a line of oaks on the right to a stile. Cross a field diagonally right, passing a copse on the left, to a stile on the right at the top of the field. Over the stile turn left and follow a left-hand boundary across two fields. Turn sharp left up a field to a stile and a path to the car park.

28. Ashdown Forest

Route: A superb walk with magnificent views. The paths gradually rise and fall throughout but none are difficult. There are no signposts in the forest because the paths are permissive and not rights of way. However, as most of them are wide tracks, with a little care there should be no problems.

Teashop: Duddleswell Tea Rooms is the only teashop in the forest, therefore it isvery busy, especially at weekends. There is seating outside – also a pleasant green for when all the seats are taken! Excellent food is served with speed and efficiency by friendly staff. Open February to November, Tuesday to Sunday 10.00am – 5.00pm. Tel: 01825 712126

Distance: 5½ miles.

How to get there: From East Grinstead follow the A22 to Forest Row. Turn left onto the B2110 and right at the B2026. After approximately 4 miles turn right into Stonehill Road.

Public Transport: Bus services: Stagecoach South Coast, Brighton & Hove.

Start: GR 462286. The Hollies car park Stonehill Road.

Maps: Landranger 188 & 187, Explorer 135(18), Pathfinder 1269 TQ42/52.

Ashdown Forest once comprised 15,000 acres. In the Middle Ages it supplied 'pannage' (acorns and beechmast) for 7,000 pigs; a scant livelihood for charcoal burners and timber for shipbuilding. For 300 years, from the early 1300s, it was a royal hunting ground. During the 1600s over half the forest was taken for land enclosure. Today, rising over 700 feet (213m), the forest comprises 6,500 acres of woodland and open heathland. In 1974 the Ashdown Forest Act gave the public right of access on foot throughout the forest.

The forest is one of the few remaining areas of lowland heath in Europe. Now that commoners no longer exercise their rights to graze there is danger of bracken, birch and Scots pine taking over from the valuable heathers: resulting in a loss of important habitat for many unique species of flora and fauna; the forest therefore has to be managed. The Board of Conservators and a team of volunteers are constantly employed controlling the unwanted vegetation and encouraging the recolonization of heather.

Whether ablaze with gorse, heather, amazing autumn colours or even in winter when covered in snow, the forest is a delight to explore.

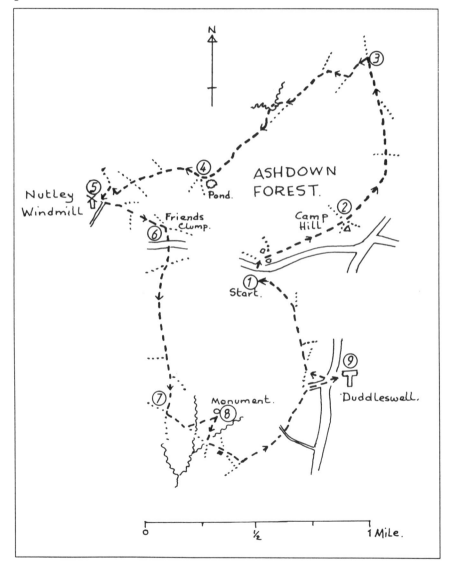

1. Cross the road into Ellisons Pond car park. Follow a wide track on the right, first between ponds then uphill to Camp Hill Clump.

   In 1825 the Lady of the Manor of Duddleswell planted eight clumps of Scots pine on the heights of the forest, as a landscape feature for the public to enjoy. The right to visit these clumps was the only public right of access over much of the forest prior to the 1974 Act. Unfortunately, her act of goodwill was unappreciated by many of the local people, who preferred the open heathland and the sparse oak and beech. From Camp Hill are magnificent views across the forest to the South Downs.

2. Take a wide descending track opposite the wooden Camp Hill Clump sign. The track contours the crest of the valley parallel to the road. Shortly ignore what appears to be a first crossing path and continue ahead to a wide grassy path coming in at an angle from the right. 250 metres beyond this path a crossing path is reached.

3. Turn left to begin descending through the valley. Bear right at a fork, soon cross a small plank footbridge and turn left onto a broad track. Bear right at a sign stating "This ride is closed". The path dips to the left and crosses a small stream at a pretty spot known locally as 'The Garden of Eden'. Continue up the path, rejoin the main track and turn right. Eventually the track passes a small pond on the left in a hollow.

4. Immediately beyond the pond turn right. The track gently undulates to a crossing path at which point it ascends steeply to a T-junction. Turn right for 60 metres to a narrow path on the left leading up to Nutley Windmill.

   After lying idle for over 60 years, Nutley Windmill was restored in 1969 by the Nutley Preservation Society. Today it is the oldest working post mill in Sussex. It is open the last Sunday of each month and Bank Holidays from 2.30pm – 5.30pm.

   Friend's Clump was planted in 1973 by the Friends of Ashdown Forest to celebrate Tree Planting Year.

5. From the windmill go through a gate on the left of a cottage and

Nutley windmill

follow a narrow path back to the main track. Continue ahead to Friend's Clump.

6. Turn right to cross a car park and the road into Stonehill car park. Cross onto a descending grassy path in the bottom left-hand corner. At a wide grassy path cross diagonally right onto a wide track for a beautiful walk through the valley. The track descends between birch, stunted oak, bracken and heather and there are superb views to the distant South Downs.

7. On reaching a wide crossing path turn left (on turning you will see a barn roof showing above the trees in the distance). Bear left after 75 metres and descend to first cross a stream then ascend to the Airmen's Memorial.

This simple memorial marks the spot where a Wellington bomber crashed in the summer of 1941 and the crew of six were all killed. The memorial was erected by the mother of the second pilot. A service is held each year on Remembrance Sunday when many ramblers and horse-riders assemble to pay their respects.

8. With your back to the memorial take a broad track downhill. Cross a footbridge on the left and turn left uphill: the track eventually levels out and passes barns on the right. From the barns take the track bearing left (marked horses). At a crossing track turn left along a broad track. Cross a lane and continue ahead until reaching another lane. Turn right to the main road. Turn left to the tea shop.

9. From the tea shop cross into Duddleswell car park. Follow a path at the rear which leads to a wide track. Turn right. Ignore a right fork after 30 metres and continue along the main track which dips then rises and curves right. On reaching a gate to a riding school on the right, continue to the left to descend to Hollies car park.

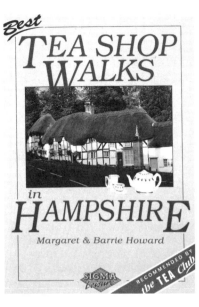

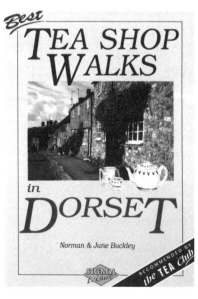

More Tea Shop Walks to Savour!

The Sigma Leisure 'Best Tea Shop Walks' series already includes:

Cheshire

Chilterns

Dorset

Hampshire

Cotswolds

Lake District, Volume 1

Lake District, Volume 2

Lancashire

Leicestershire & Rutland

North Devon

Oxfordshire

Peak District

Shropshire

Snowdonia

South Devon & Dartmoor

Staffordshire

Warwickshire

Worcestershire

Yorkshire Dales

Each book costs £6.95 and contains an average of 25 excellent walks – far better value than any competitor!

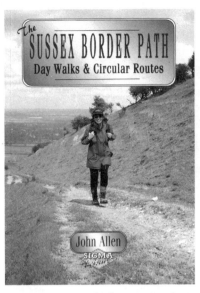
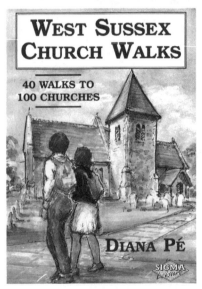